Praise for the nature classic **Where the Sea Breaks Its Back:**

"In the history of maritime discovery, few voyages can match the obstacles, hardships and success of Bering's Second Expedition in 1741, that initial crossing of the North Pacific. *Where the Sea Breaks Its Back* tells the heroic and tragic story of that momentous expedition. The book's hero is not Vitus Bering, the commander who died at the moment before success, but Georg Wilhelm Steller, the brilliant German-born scientist, naturalist, botanist and physician who accompanied Bering.

"Corey Ford skillfully unfolds Steller's complex, contradictory nature and the significance of the events in which he figured....The book...will appeal...to all who want a true story well told."   *—The New York Times*

"While essentially the book is a testament to the human spirit, Ford's concern for the lesser creatures, the unique wildlife in this part of the world, runs as an enlightening and important undercurrent."   *—Chicago Tribune*

"[The chapter called] *'The Plunderers'*—the horrifying account of the near-extinction of the sea otter by Russian fur traders in the mid-eighteenth century in the Aleutian Islands, and later measures taken to save the animals—[is] a classic story of conservation."   *—Field & Stream*

"*Where the Sea Breaks Its Back* is more than a thrilling adventure story. It is a vivid word picture of Alaska's pioneer naturalist, and of the strange birds and beasts of the sea which he observed in the fogbound and mysterious Aleutian chain. Here is a solid contribution to American natural history...."
**—from the Introduction by Frank Dufresne,
former Director, Alaska Game Commission**

Where the Sea Breaks
Its Back

*The Epic Story of Early Naturalist Georg Steller
and the Russian Exploration of Alaska*

by COREY FORD

With drawings by LOIS DARLING

ALASKA NORTHWEST BOOKS™

Anchorage • Portland

FIRST ALASKA NORTHWEST BOOKS™ PRINTING: 1992
FOURTH ALASKA NORTHWEST BOOKS™ PRINTING: 2000

LIBRARY OF CONGRESS CATALOGING-IN-PUBLICATION DATA

FORD, COREY, 1902–1969
WHERE THE SEA BREAKS ITS BACK: THE EPIC STORY OF EARLY NATURALIST GEORG STELLER AND THE RUSSIAN EXPLORATION OF ALASKA / BY COREY FORD: WITH DRAWINGS BY LOIS DARLING.
P.   CM.
ORIGINALLY PUBLISHED: BOSTON: LITTLE, BROWN, 1966.
INCLUDES BIBLIOGRAPHICAL REFERENCES.
ISBN: 0-88240-394-X
1. STELLER, GEORG WILHELM, 1709–1746—JOURNEYS—ALASKA.
2. KAMCHATSKAIA EXSPEDITSHA (2ND: 1733–1743). 3. RUSSIANS—ALASKA—HISTORY—18TH CENTURY. 4. ALASKA—DISCOVERY AND EXPLORATION—18TH CENTURY. 5. NATURALISTS—GERMANY—BIBLIOGRAPHY. I. TITLE.
QH31.S65F6   1992
508.798′092—DC20
[B]   92-3387
                                                           CIP

WHERE THE SEA BREAKS ITS BACK WAS FIRST PUBLISHED IN 1966 BY LITTLE, BROWN AND COMPANY, IN BOSTON AND SIMULTANEOUSLY IN TORONTO, CANADA. THE TEXT OF THE 1992 EDITION WAS PUBLISHED BY ARRANGEMENT WITH HAROLD OBER ASSOCIATES, INC., NEW YORK. ORIGINAL ILLUSTRATIONS BY LOIS DARLING WERE PUBLISHED BY ARRANGEMENT WITH LITTLE, BROWN AND COMPANY.

FRONT COVER, 19TH CENTURY ENGRAVING:
Vitus Bering Discovers Alaska and Perishes in Ice-Bound Seas
COURTESY THE BETTMANN ARCHIVE
COVER DESIGN BY KATE L. THOMPSON

ALASKA NORTHWEST BOOKS™
An imprint of Graphics Arts Center Publishing Company
P.O. BOX 10306, PORTLAND, OR 97296-0306
503-226-2402; www.gacpc.com

PRINTED ON ACID-FREE RECYCLED PAPER IN THE UNITED STATES OF AMERICA

In Memory of
Frank Dufresne

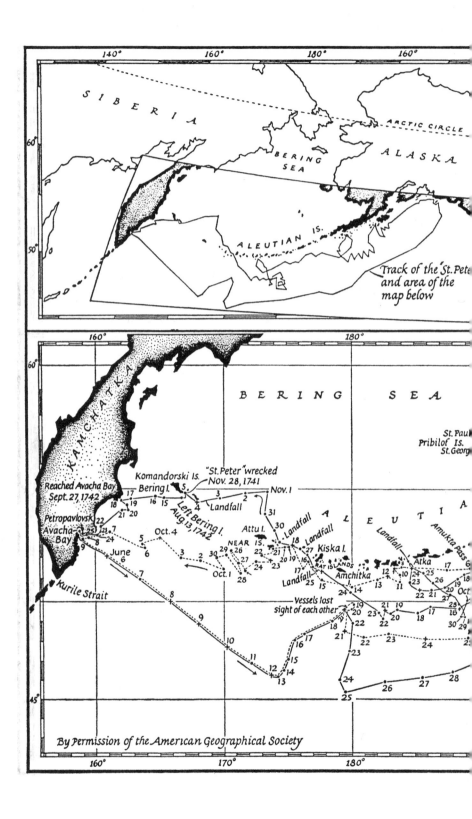

By Permission of the American Geographical Society

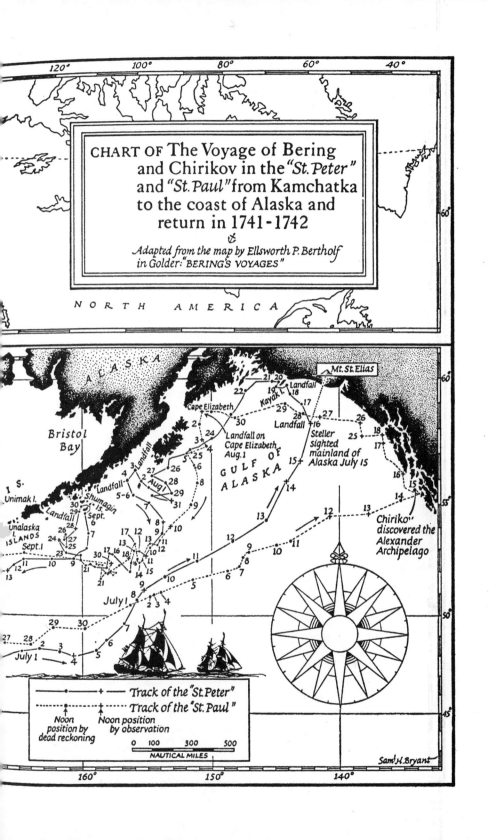

CHART OF The Voyage of Bering and Chirikov in the "St. Peter" and "St. Paul" from Kamchatka to the coast of Alaska and return in 1741-1742

Adapted from the map by Ellsworth P. Bertholf in Golder: "BERING'S VOYAGES"

—•——+—— Track of the "St. Peter"
·········†········ Track of the "St. Paul"

Noon position by dead reckoning
Noon position by observation

0   100   300   500
NAUTICAL MILES

Sam. H. Bryant

Introduction

G EORG WILHELM STELLER was one of the strangest and most fascinating characters ever to appear on the western scene. He was brilliant; he was arrogant; he was gifted as are few men. Though he spent no more than ten hours on Alaskan soil, his accomplishments in that short day were such that his name will live forever. There is nothing comparable to his deeds — nor to Steller, the man — in all our history.

He was naturalist, botanist, physician. All three professions played important parts in his meteoric career. As a naturalist, on Vitus Bering's historic voyage to Alaska in 1741, he discovered the Steller's Jay, the Steller's Eider, the rare Steller's Eagle, and the now legendary Steller's White Raven. Turning to the ocean, he found and recorded the Steller's Greenling, our brilliantly colored rock trout. His is the only description of the giant northern manatee called Steller's Sea Cow, which became totally extinct shortly afterward. Stranger still is his detailed report of a creature never again seen by man: Steller's Sea Monkey, which lives only in this young German's vivid field notes. Steller's Hill on Kayak Island, Steller's Mountain, and Steller's Arch are visible monuments to the first white man ever to set foot in northwest America, the first naturalist to describe the flora and fauna of the new world.

As a botanist, Georg Wilhelm Steller collected and classified scores of hitherto unknown plants. It was his knowledge of their antiscorbutic value, combined with his devoted skill as a physician, which saved the lives of his Russian shipmates as they lay dying beside their wrecked vessel on a lonely island in Bering Sea. Though he professed only contempt for these ignorant sailors, and castigated them pitilessly aboard ship, he tended them like babies when they cried out for help.

Steller, the man, was so complex as to defy analysis. You could hate him, you could love him, but you could never understand him. The writer who has come closest to bringing back a living Steller for you to meet, and judge for yourself, is Corey Ford.

Two hundred years after Georg Steller, almost to the day, Corey Ford — himself a highly qualified naturalist and historian — sailed the stormy waters of the North Pacific on a course remarkably coincidental with that of Bering's ill-fated *St. Peter*. He visited the same Aleutian Islands, saw the same birds and mammals, and experienced the same violent gales and fog in a remote region which has altered but little in two centuries. With Steller's own journal in his hands, Corey Ford compared, caught fire, became fascinated. This book is the result.

Where the Sea Breaks Its Back is more than a thrilling adventure story. It is a vivid word picture of Alaska's pioneer naturalist, and of the strange birds and beasts of the sea which he observed in the fogbound and mysterious Aleutian chain. Here is a solid contribution to American natural history, as well as an important restoration of our nation's neglected past.

FRANK DUFRESNE
Former Director,
Alaska Game Commission

Contents

PART ONE

Volcanoes, Mummies, Sea Otters

YEARS AGO, when I was very young, I crossed the North Pacific from Vancouver to Japan; and one day, as our ship rounded the top of the great circle, I noticed a string of strange bare mountains rising out of the sea along the northern horizon. They resembled heaps of smoking slag; the sun, striking their sides, gave them a greenish cast like verdigris on copper. I asked a fellow passenger what they were. "Illusions," I thought he said, but now I realize he said they were the Aleutians.

They were still illusory and unreal when I saw them for a second time in 1941, aboard the Alaska Game Commission

cruiser *Brown Bear* on a survey count of sea otters in the islands. Dim eldritch forms would loom without warning out of
the fog, their rocky promontories boiling with surf, the cliffs
spattered with the lime of a million sea birds and carved into
fantastic arches and grottoes by the ceaseless abrasion of the
waves. Sometimes a half-submerged reef would bare its teeth
for a moment in the trough of a swell; sometimes, when the
Brown Bear entered a hidden bay, a number of weird mush-
room-shaped rocks would appear solemnly on all sides of us,
like a troop of goblins come out from shore to inspect this
intruder in their solitary domain. "Pinnacle rocks," Captain
John Sellevold would mutter. "Don't even show on the chart."

Captain John was a tall grave man, taciturn, friendly in a
shy intuitive way. His lean face was a geometry of planes and
ridges, with hollow sockets from which his eyes peered with a
hard brilliance. He navigated by a sort of sixth sense, steering
unerringly through tortuous channels and past reefs that
lurked in wait in the blinding mist and rain. Often we could
not see the bow of the boat from the pilothouse; we had to
grope our way, giving a blast every so often on the whistle and
judging by its echo how far we were from shore. The best
available government maps were incomplete, dotted with submerged shoals marked P.D. — position doubtful — or in-
scribed with the routine warning: "This position may be two
miles off." Some of the bays in which the *Brown Bear* anchored were not on any map at all. Here and there a headland
would bear an odd name: Martha, Star of Bengal, Oneida.
"They were ships," Captain John said briefly.

I spent much of my time in the pilothouse, studying the incredible concentration of waterfowl in the Aleutians. The
show of birds was beyond belief. The sea, the land, the sky
were constantly stirring with wings. An entire white cliff

would explode before my eyes into a swarm of Pacific kittiwakes, their snowy plumage and solid black wingtips blinking
like a camera shutter. Murres would pitch from their nests on
the ledges as the *Brown Bear* approached, to dive into the
ocean beside us and, literally flying under water with short-
ened wing strokes, come up on the other side of the boat and
emerge at full speed. Tiny crested auklets hovered and danced
offshore like clouds of midges; Pacific fulmars and petrels and
glaucous-winged gulls, loveliest of all seagulls, were everywhere in fantastic numbers; sooty albatross would skim the
tops of the combers hour after hour in our wake. Slender-
billed shearwaters — the famous muttonbirds of Tasmania
and the South Seas, which nest each winter on the rim of the
Antarctic ice pack and perversely migrate north to the Aleutians each summer — would settle and rock easily on the
waves: solid brown acres of them, mile after mile, feeding on
the plankton churned up by the tide rips. Now and then a fat
worried puffin would scurry across our bows, beating its
stubby wings on the water and voiding as it sought to unload
ballast and take to the air.

Captain John jerked his head, without taking his eyes off
our course, to indicate a snow-capped peak on the horizon,
from which a steady cloud bent at an angle. "Kiska Volcano.
All these islands are sunken volcanoes." A smile warmed his
curt clipped speech. "We sail right over the tops of some of
them."

These exposed rocks had been mountain peaks once, these
reefs over which the surf was curling and seething were the
rims of extinct craters. Back in prehistoric times a majestic
range linked the American continent with Asia, before it foundered and sank in some cataclysmic upheaval. The ocean rose
beyond timberline, and only a few smoking summits remained

above the waves. I thought of the former verdant valleys buried under tons of green water now, populated by shadowy popeyed fish which cruise their drowned and silent forests.

The Aleutian chain is one of the loneliest and least-known spots on earth. Think of Alaska as a profile of Uncle Sam; the Seward Peninsula forms his angular nose, the Alaska Peninsula is the point of his jutting jaw, and his chin-whiskers waggle across the Pacific almost to Asia. Unimak Island, at the beginning of the chain, is five hundred miles farther west than Hawaii; the Andreanofs are due north of New Zealand; and Attu, westernmost point of the American continent, is only a few hundred miles from Kamchatka. In the entire thousand-mile stretch there is no tree or shrub higher than your knee, nothing but bare hills and beaches purple with volcanic cinders, fogbound and cold and still as death.

The islands have always been a link between two worlds. Over this ancient landbridge, it is believed, nomadic tribes from Asia and even Africa migrated to the American mainland. The native Aleuts are supposed to be descendants of the Hairy Ainus, original inhabitants of the island of Nippon, who were driven from their homeland by swart barbarians from the south called Japanese. They settled in the Aleutians, living in sod-covered *barabaras* with giant whale ribs for rafters, hunting seals and sea lions and using sea otter fur for their clothing. Invading Koryaks from Kamchatka and Chukchis from northeast Siberia — ancestors of the Alaska Eskimos — descended upon the islands in their skin *baidarkas*, slaughtering the peaceful Aleuts and burning their homes; and new civilizations rose on the ashes of the old. Beneath a long-obliterated village site, overgrown with rye grass or buried under the debris of a volcanic eruption, can be found the traces of earlier cultures, layer on successive layer, like volumes in a set of history. Archaeologists, digging through the clutter of shells and fishbones and charred sections of whale vertebrae in a kitchen midden, may overturn broken bits of pottery, beads, stone hatchets, occasionally a beautifully carved ivory labret worn as an ornament through the pierced cheek of some forgotten chieftain. During World War II a group of enlisted men, burying a fuel tank in the hillside behind Dutch Harbor, uncovered a circle of twenty-seven human skeletons arranged in a timeless council.

Mostly the early tribes buried their warrior-dead in the labyrinthine caves around the bases of the volcanoes. The bodies were carefully eviscerated, stuffed with wild rye (*elymus*) and placed in a sitting position, the knees drawn up under the chin, the arms folded, the head bent forward in an attitude of brooding contemplation. The natural heat of the volcano dried and preserved the mummies; landslides and geologic disturbances sealed the entrances to the caves and locked away their secrets forever. Where this process of mummification originated is not known. The late Dr. Aleš Hrdlička, curator of anthropology in the Smithsonian Institution, estimated their age to be more than thirty-five hundred years and claimed the art was practiced in only two widely separated places in America: the Aleutians and Peru. Perhaps the original secret was brought by wanderers from Egypt who crossed the landbridge and migrated down the west coast of the continent to South America.

An earlier expedition of the Alaska Game Commission, on a similar summer count of the sea otter herds, discovered quite by accident the largest collection of mummies in the Aleutians. The party had been gathering bird specimens on Kagamil Island, in the Four Mountain Group, and as they were returning to the *Brown Bear*, working their way back along the south shore of the island, they heard a blue fox barking at them from a cave some fifty yards above the water. They marked the location by a live fumarole which was sending a steady jet of steam through a fissure in the rocks beside the cave, and climbed the loose mass of tumbled boulders to the entrance, a narrow V-shaped orifice. Mingled with the sulphurous odor of the fumarole was a curious death smell which issued from the mouth of the cave. The fox had fled, but the object on which it had been chewing lay at their feet. It was a section of a human arm.

Laboriously they wriggled and squeezed feet first into the vault. The ceiling was so low they could not stand upright, and caked with a hard white mineral deposit. The floor was littered with rubble, loose rocks, pieces of bone, the scat of numerous foxes, all of it covered with a fine fluffy brown dust, as soft as lint, which rose around their boots as they crept forward. It was uncomfortably warm in the cave — the dirt in places was actually too hot to touch — and the strange fetid smell gagged them. They crawled in single file on their hands and knees, hugging the wall for guidance in the pitch blackness. Abruptly the leader halted with a gasp of fright. A hand reaching from the wall had raked its fingers across his cheek.

He struck a match. Before him, in the flickering light, he saw the withered arm of a mummy protruding from the dirt. It had been partly dug out of its earthly tomb by the ravenous foxes; the exposed portion of its leathery face had been eaten away, but the part still buried was intact.

The match went out; someone lit a second. Beyond them they made out another sunken grinning face, and still another. Both sides of the cave were lined with dry bodies, as far as they could see. Once they had been stacked in tiers, one upon another, supported by racks of driftwood. Most of them had been dislodged and violated by the foxes, and one or two mummies had been dragged onto the floor of the cave. They were of all ages: adult males and females, children, even a premature birth in a basket of pleated grass. Each body had been clothed in otter fur or a bird-skin parka, and wrapped in sea lion hide which was laced together with thongs of twisted kelp. They wore ivory ornaments around their necks and in their cheeks; one wrinkled monkey-face had a jaunty feather stuck through the lobe of his left ear.

All around them were crude artifacts, torn matting, shreds of woven mummy wrappings, bones, trinkets. Part of a skin kayak, interred with its owner, lay overturned on its side; paddles, war shields, stone lamps, delicate grass baskets were spilled in the dust. Still buried in the wall was a carved wooden dish, filled with the dried wings of birds, probably a funeral offering; an ornithologist in the party recognized the feathers of the pine grosbeak. A solitary skull lay in a wicker basket lined with moss, shiny as an Easter egg, the top of the head neatly split by a stone axe.

I saw some of the specimens later in the Smithsonian Museum in Washington. The old boy with the feather in his ear grinned at me from his glass case; beside him hung a shrunken Jívaro head from Peru, a similar feather thrust through his left earlobe — further evidence of the link between the two remote cultures. Dr. Hrdlička showed me a Peruvian wooden doll and a splintered portion of one from the Aleutians. They were almost identical in appearance. If he could ever find a whole Aleutian doll, Dr. Hrdlička said, he was sure he could establish the truth of his theory.

I recalled his remark during the war, when I touched briefly at Dutch Harbor on my way down the Aleutians to join the Air Force bomber unit to which I had been assigned. A sergeant from Minnesota had been excavating for a gun emplacement, he told me, and his shovel had overturned a dozen wooden dolls in perfect condition. From his description, they were the same as the Peruvian doll I had seen in the Smithsonian. Here was the proof that anthropologists had awaited so long. "Where are they now, sergeant?"

"I sent 'em back to my little daughter in Minnesota, sir, she's fond of dolls," he said. "She never got the package, though. Prolly lost in the mails . . ."

The name Alaska is probably an abbreviation of Unalaska, derived from the original Aleut word *agunalaksh*, which means "the shores where the sea breaks its back." The war between water and land is never-ending. Waves shatter themselves in spent fury against the rocky bulwarks of the coast; giant tides eat away the sand beaches and alter the entire contour of an island overnight; williwaw winds pour down the side of a volcano like snow sliding off a roof, building to a hundred-mile velocity in a matter of minutes and churning the ocean into a maelstrom where the stoutest vessels founder.

Here is the very breeding ground of storms. Cold air blowing off the Siberian land mass strikes the moisture-laden air of the warm Japanese current; the cauldron bubbles and boils, and a succession of lows, like jets of steam from a tea kettle, shoot eastward along the Aleutian chain. During the two months that the *Brown Bear* cruised these waters, we counted only six clear days. Week after week the clouds hid the horizon, and there was nothing but wind and driving rain and the immense empty ocean.

Captain John dropped anchor in Kiska harbor on one of the rare sunny days of the summer, and Alaska Wildlife Agent Douglas Gray and I hurried ashore to look for sea otters. We left the dinghy and started east along the beach, scanning the kelp beds for any sign of life. The black sand was strewn with chunks of lava, strands of kelp as thick as hawsers, occasional green glass floats that had broken loose from Japanese fishing nets and washed ashore. A matted line of driftwood marked high water, and beyond it was an almost tropical growth of giant rye, the stalks braided by the wind into a hopeless tangle. We had to force our way step by step through the lush grass. Gradually it began to thin, yielding to a spongy moss, and we emerged at last onto the rolling tundra that covered the lower slopes of the mountain. It was a gay lilliputian meadow, dotted with dwarfed flowers and stunted willows only a couple of feet high, bent at an angle by the prevailing wind. Higher on the slopes the moss disappeared, and the shoulders of Kiska Volcano emerged, blown bare of all topsoil, stark and forbidding.

Even on the tundra the going was difficult, and my boots sank clear to the ankles in the soft wet bog of Salmon Lagoon. Here we found two abandoned trappers' cabins; the only human touch was a homemade mandolin fashioned out of a cigar box and wire. (There was no sign of the cabins when I looked down on Kiska two years later through a bomber's plexiglas window.) We followed the rim of a high fluted cliff, overlooking the water. A thousand feet below us, the surf broke on the beach with a deep bell-note, and a few sea lions, like bloated wine sacks, were basking on the sand. We swept our glasses over the kelp beds, but they were deserted.

The sun was setting; we watched it poise on the horizon and then slip out of sight as deftly as a conjurer's coin. A queer chuckling sound caught our ears, and we halted. A small dark-bodied bird, with white eyes and a crested topknot like a California quail, marched out from a crevice in the cliff and regarded us owlishly for a moment. Then he fluffed his feathers — I could have sworn he shrugged — and walked to the end of a projecting rock, and pitched in a power dive toward the water. Through my glasses I saw him spread his wings and level off at the bottom of his descent, only a few inches from the surface of the ocean, and shoot out at right angles like a projectile from a gun.

He was followed by a steady succession of other birds, each in turn stepping out onto a rock and hurtling down in the same breathtaking leap. Some were crested auklets; some the absurd-looking least auklet, its big eyes surrounded by a few scattered white bristles, giving the effect of plucked eyebrows; some the rare rhinoceros auklet with a tuft of feathers sprouting from its bill like a horn. The air was full of acrobatic birds, forming single lines and moving in long undulating ribbons below us, crisscrossing each other's paths, weaving in and out in graceful patterns, alternately light and dark as they turned in the air. Abruptly the show ended. At some inaudible signal, the ribbons wound upward to the top of the cliff, and with a roar like a waterfall the entire flock disintegrated overhead and landed all about us. One by one they gave us the same owlish look, shrugged again, and trudged back into their burrows for the night.

We set out next morning in a depressing drizzle, this time heading westward. The character of the island seemed to change; the slopes grew more precipitous, and deep gullies blocked our way. We were forced to abandon the green uplands and clamber down a crumbling cliff to the water's edge. The narrow beach was a mass of round boulders, covered with slippery kelp, and we had to hop from rock to rock over the intervening leads of dark heaving water. Giant beach fleas, capable of stripping a stranded carcass overnight, leapt like grasshoppers along the sand ahead of us. Hordes of gnats burned our ears and cheeks, and perspiration ran saltily into our eyes.

The substance of the entire cliff was lava. Beneath it the bloodstream of the old volcano still ran hot; steam jets rose from the black rocks, little boiling streams ran down the face of the cliff to the sea, and here and there a sulphur spring bubbled up between the boulders. The beach was desolate and somehow sinister. Murres, disturbed in their brooding, wheeled screaming overhead, and glaucous-winged gulls took advantage of their alarm to snatch the downy fledglings from the nests. Red-legged oyster catchers shrilled at us as we passed. Occasionally a fat tufted puffin would take off from shore and pedal industriously in a long futile circle back to the very spot he had started from, his white side-whiskers streaming behind him, like a black-frocked English vicar doing his parish rounds on a bicycle.

I was beginning to feel the utter loneliness of the islands. The mist was still falling, clammy and cold; it cut to the bone as we reached the windswept point. We crept around it cautiously, keeping out of sight behind the ledges. Loose volcanic cinders revolved underfoot, and our footprints vanished as though we were walking in water. The silence was disturbed only by the strident gulls, the steady rumble of surf, the exploding pop of a bladder of seaweed beneath our boots. Doug Gray crouched suddenly and held up his hand. "There. In front of you."

All I could see was the ocean and the long sleek ropes of kelp, moving up and down gently as the Pacific swells flattened hissing on the sand. And then I made out something else: first a tiny speck, then larger, then clearly the outline of an animal moving toward me. Slowly, at a steady pace, the otter came nearer, swimming on its back: a habit of this fabulous animal that is half of the land and half of the sea. Now I could see its triangular head, its wizened wise teddy-bear face, the black cloverleaf flippers with which it kicked itself past the rocks where we lay hidden. Cradled on its chest, held securely in its forepaws, was a baby otter, which the mother rocked gently as she swam. She paused in front of us, rolled the baby off her chest onto a bed of kelp — "the young ones," Gray whispered, "don't know how to swim" — and swirled and dove with a single powerful kick of her flippers.

She came up a moment later, clutching a sea urchin in her paws. Holding its spiny shell between the calloused pads, she mashed it and spread the orange-colored glob of meat on her furry chest. With great delicacy she began to feed morsels to the young otter on the kelp bed; he took the pieces in his own little forepaws and devoured them hungrily. The meal finished, she picked the last crumbs from her fur and nibbled on them, brushed away the empty bits of shell, and lifted the baby back onto her chest. They drifted past us, less than fifty feet away, and I could see her eyes gazing moodily at the gray sky, her body rising and falling with the waves, for all the world like a matron and her offspring basking in the ocean at Asbury Park. As I watched, she crossed one black flipper over the other and wriggled the tips luxuriously, as though she had kicked off her bathing shoes and were working her bare toes in the water.

Perhaps I moved; perhaps a stray filament of scent carried out to her. She stood on end in the water like a gopher, craning her neck as she stared toward shore; then, with an alarmed hiss, she grabbed the baby in her teeth by the nape of its neck and began to swim rapidly away, huffing and blowing out her mustache. Occasionally she would pause, rearing again and shading her eyes with a forepaw as she peered back at us, until she was lost in the fog.

The sea otter has good reason to fear humans; for this bewhiskered Old Man of the Sea happens to be cursed with the most beautiful fur in the world. So highly was it prized by the early Chinese mandarins that at one time a single skin would bring as high as five thousand dollars. It was the quest for this coveted pelt, rather than for gold, which lured the Russian adventurers to Alaska and the Pacific Northwest, and ushered in two centuries of plunder and bloodshed which brought the otter herds to the verge of extinction and virtually wiped out the native Aleut race.

The sea otter has two distinct color phases: one a dark ash brown with a sprinkling of gold, the other and more valuable a blue-black star-dusted with silver guard hairs which increase from the shoulders forward, giving the neck and head a grizzled gray cast. Unlike almost any other animal except the fur seal, its coat is prime the year round. It lies on the otter in soft folds, loosely furled; you can stretch a pelt a third again its normal size, and still you cannot force your fingers down through the hair and touch the hide.

Ceaseless persecution has honed the otter's senses to a razor sharpness; its scent is perhaps the keenest of any wild creature. When the breeze is right, it can detect an intruder a couple of miles away. It feeds entirely in the water, diving to a depth of a hundred and fifty feet for food. Its main diet is sea urchins, small crustaceans which fasten themselves to rocks underwater in bright-colored beds, and protect themselves from enemies by means of sharp spines and the Latin name *strongylocentrotus drobachiensis*. Only the sea otter, with its hard clublike paws, can crack the urchin's spiky armor. The otter also enjoys an occasional shore dinner of limpets, periwinkles, crabs, seaweed, and small red chitons — tough leathery mollusks called *baidarkas* by the Aleuts because of their boatlike shape. An otter will clamp its teeth on one of these chitons and tug until it bites out a mouthful, like a chaw of cut plug. Usually after a full meal it takes a siesta in the surf, wrapping a strand of kelp around its middle to keep it from drifting, and slumbering on its back in the lazy swells.

Even when it is asleep, its uncannily sharp senses are aware of the least suspicious sound. Once I crept within a hundred feet of a dozing otter with a face which reminded me of the late W. C. Fields. At the first faint click of my camera it opened its eyes and swung its head around sharply, like an old gentleman surprised in the bathtub. It cast one exasperated look in my direction, revolved to free itself from its kelp harness, and plunged out of sight with a final indignant snort.

"Altogether [the sea otter is] a beautiful and pleasing animal," Georg Wilhelm Steller wrote in 1742, "cunning and amusing in its habits, and at the same time ingratiating and amorous. They prefer to lie together in families, the male with its mate, the half-grown young and the very young sucklings all together. The male caresses the female by stroking her, using the forefeet as hands, and places himself over her; she, however, often pushes him away from her for fun and in simulated coyness, as it were, and plays with her offspring like the fondest mother. Their love for their young is so intense that they expose themselves to the most manifest danger of death. When [their young are] taken away from them, they cry bitterly, like a small child, and grieve so much that, as we have observed from rather authentic cases, after ten to fourteen days they grow as lean as a skeleton, become sick and feeble, and will not leave the shore."

When I boarded the *Brown Bear* that summer, I brought with me the two volumes of F. A. Golder's *Bering's Voyages*, published in 1925 by the American Geographical Society. One volume contains the ship's log of the *St. Peter* during Bering's expedition to Alaska. The other reprints, for the first time in English, Steller's complete journal of the tragic voyage, written when he was only thirty-three. The journal had been edited and published in German in 1793 by Steller's admirer and fellow naturalist P. S. Pallas; but Pallas had taken considerable liberties in abridging the text and deleting certain sections which he felt at the time were too controversial. For almost two centuries the original unexpurgated manuscript had lain buried in the dusty archives of the Russian Academy of Sciences in St. Petersburg (now Leningrad), until Dr. Golder discovered it. The translation, made at his request by Leonhard Stejneger of the United States National Museum, retains the full flavor of Steller's penetrating and poisonous pen.

I followed the entries day by day as we traveled westward along the Aleutian chain, sailing the very course that Vitus Bering's vessel had taken in 1741 — by an odd coincidence, exactly two hundred years later to the month and day. We touched at all the spots which Steller observed on his journey: Kayak Island and Cape St. Elias; the Shumagin Islands; Adak and Atka and Amchitka, Kiska and Buldir. The islands had not changed since he saw them; the same rugged promontories and hidden reefs, the kelp-strewn beaches, the interminable rain and fog and mystery.

I suppose it was bound to happen. As I read Steller's journal, still vivid with excitement and outrage after two centuries, I began to feel a close personal identification with the enigmatic young German naturalist. After all, there was a difference of only a few years in our ages. I found myself sharing vicariously in his emotions, scanning the ocean with his eyes, experiencing his own consuming curiosity whenever we dropped anchor on a new harbor. I would be as eager as Steller to be ashore, to leave the first footprints on the trackless sand. And I could understand his frustration when Captain John, a Scandinavian like Bering, refused to steer the *Brown Bear* closer to some uncharted headland. Captain John had Bering's innate prudence and a mariner's distrust of land; his duty was to bring his ship safely home; and I would fret and fume like Steller as the magic shore fell away behind me and was lost in the fog.

His journal reveals his complex and contradictory nature: hypersensitive himself and yet insensitive to the feelings of others, indefatigable and brilliant but dogmatic and without tact, an irascible genius who lacked the saving grace of humility, and who was unable to tolerate any difference of opinion. In his impatience to observe the natural wonders of the new continent, he could not brook interference or delay. He had no sense of fear, and resented the overcaution which Bering displayed. His opinionated manner, his shrill insistence on being heard, aroused the antagonism of his Russian shipmates, and they came in time to ignore him. He was that most thwarted of human beings, a man who knows he is right and who sees his advice ridiculed and rejected.

He possessed an extraordinary ability to observe every facet of wildlife, to commit the details to his uncanny memory, and to identify and catalog his discoveries with painstaking thoroughness and accuracy. His descriptions of the flora and fauna of the new continent, recorded in Latin in a crude sailcloth-covered shelter on Bering Island, have never been surpassed. No man ever again will have his unique opportunity to study the fur seals and sea lions and sea otters of the fogbound Aleutians before they were disturbed by man. His treatise on the giant sea cow which bears his name is the only existing account of that fabulous creature. Linnaeus, the great Swedish botanist and a contemporary of Steller, called him "the born collector of plants" and proposed the name *Stellera* to honor the devoted young scientist "who deserves so well of our world, and who has discovered so many new plants during so many years of most laborious travel. Who has earned a greater or more precious glory for his name than he who undertakes journeys among the barbarians?"

Steller was first and last a naturalist, and it was his total dedication to his calling which led him to undergo hunger and cold and shipwreck during Bering's expedition to Bolshaya Zemlya, the Great Land, which we now call Alaska. He wrote of himself once: "I have fallen in love with nature." That love sustained him to the end of his brief and lonely life — a solitary falling star against the northern sky.

PART TWO

Steller

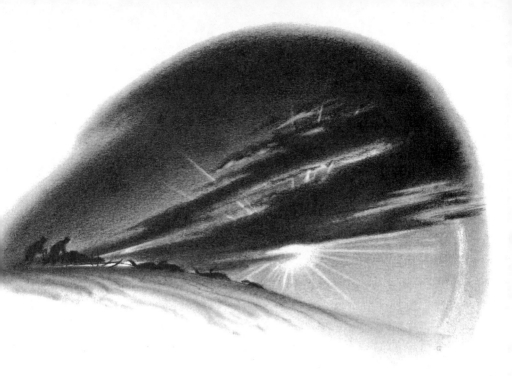

I. AVACHA BAY

KAMCHATKA PENINSULA hangs like a scimitar from the northeastern tip of Siberia, a 700-mile wilderness of smoldering volcanoes and treacherous tundra bogs. It is a land alone. To the west the Sea of Okhotsk separates it from the Asian mainland; south of it the Kurile Islands descend like steppingstones to Japan; its east coast faces the open Pacific. Arctic storms converge on its exposed flanks in winter, and life seldom stirs during the long dark months.

That spring of 1741 the snow still lay six feet deep in the interior. Drifts blocked the mountain passes, and all but buried the dense and pathless willow jungles which covered the lower plains. A buffeting March wind, howling down from the polar seas, hurled ice crystals in stinging clouds and obliterated the tracks of the solitary dogsled, mushing across the peninsula toward Avacha Bay.

Five Siberian huskies made up the team, two pairs har-
nessed side by side and the lone lead dog setting the pace. The
Kamchatka-style sled was ingeniously fashioned, a lattice-
work basket of supple wooden slats bound with rawhide
thongs and slung from four upright posts, curved like walrus
tusks. It weighed no more than sixteen pounds, and was so
strong and pliable that it could contract and squeeze through
the tangled willows, wherever the dogs found an opening. If it
skidded into a boulder or crashed against a tree, it would bend
almost double without breaking.

Steller sat sideways in the woven carriage, ready to dodge
the interlaced branches or leap off and help push the sleigh up a
steep grade. He had wrapped himself in bearskins against the
numbing cold, and protected his face by a parka hood lined with
wolverine, the only fur which the human breath does not frost.
His exposed cheeks were windburned to such a deep bronze
that he might have been mistaken for a native, save for his
blond eyebrows and Nordic blue eyes. He was dressed in a
deerskin jacket, which the Siberian squaws had cleansed of its
hair by soaking it in urine and ashes, and made soft by rubbing it with reindeer brains and tallow. A knitted wool toque
was pulled down over his straw-colored hair, and his native-
made boots had reindeer tops and sealskin bottoms with the
fur turned inside for warmth.

The pale blue eyes were never still, moving left and right
with a naturalist's keen perception, noting every detail of the
white winter world and committing it to his prodigious memory. A rock ptarmigan, which had burrowed under a snow-
bank for shelter, erupted ahead of the dogs in a feathered
explosion. Steller recalled an illustration he had seen in a textbook back in Germany, and identified it at a glance by its black
wing coverts. In the distance a dense fog bank hovered over

the willows; a herd of reindeer pawing for moss, he guessed, their warm bodies steaming in the sub-zero air. Several tan forms stood silhouetted on a ridge against the sky; *Ovis nivicola*, the Kamchatkan mountain sheep. He would set down the observations in his journal when they stopped at night to make camp.

Behind him his loyal *slushiv*, a cossack boy named Thoma Lepekhin, rode the rear of the long slim runners, only a third of an inch thick. He was a black-bearded young giant, with a powerful body and the mind of a simple child. Like most Cossacks in Siberia, he belonged to the irregular unmounted militia used by the government both in civil and military work, and Steller had taken him on as personal servant and hunter. He was devoted to his master, though they seldom spoke; Lepekhin knew no German, and Steller scorned to employ the language of the Russians, whom he regarded as little more than barbarians. The only sounds that broke the stillness were Lepekhin's guttural commands to the lead dog, and the occasional crack of his ten-foot whip over the heads of the floundering team.

It was hard going. Hollows and sudden rises were indistinguishable in the blinding whiteness, and sometimes the sleigh all but sank out of sight in the soft snow. There was no trail to follow; the only Russian settlement of any size in Kamchatka was the tiny garrison town of Bolsheretsk on the west coast, beside the Sea of Okhotsk, and the wild interior had never been mapped. A few nomadic tribes called Kamchadals trapped and fished in the southern portion of the peninsula, and in the north were the more warlike Koryaks. The natives, who were forced to pay tribute in furs to their Russian overlords, were sullen and rebellious. More than one government tax collector had disappeared in the hinterland without a trace, and Lepekhin kept his musket loaded and handy in case of ambush.

They were making slow progress, and Steller fumed with impatience. The distance across the peninsula to the Pacific side was less than a hundred and fifty miles, but already they had been ten days on the way. Recurrent blizzards held the dogs to a crawl or halted them altogether, and the travelers had to take refuge under the overturned sled until the storm was over. It would have been wiser to wait until April or even May, when the snow packs hard and there are more hours of daylight; but Steller was of no mind to delay. At Bolsheretsk late in February he had received an urgent message from Captain Commander Bering, requesting him to come to his temporary headquarters at Avacha Bay "for the purpose of discussing certain matters with him." Steller had no doubt what those matters were. Bering's Second Kamchatka Expedition was waiting for spring breakup to set sail across the uncharted North Pacific in search of Bolshaya Zemlya, the Great Land. "Perceiving at once that the intention was to persuade me to undertake the voyage to America in company with him," he wrote in his journal, "I did not hesitate long." He had planned half a lifetime for this opportunity, and he did not intend to miss it now.

Their sledge began to pick up speed as they descended the eastern slope of the peninsula. The dogs seemed to sense human habitation and broke into a steady trot, tails curled tight and heads high. On the afternoon of March 20 they crossed the last range of foothills, and below them, its frozen surface glinting in the sun, was the horseshoe-shaped indentation of Avacha Bay. The reflected light was no brighter than Steller's shining eyes. He would be the first scientist ever to set foot on the shore of the unknown continent, the first to study and record the natural wonders of Bolshaya Zemlya.

He had always had an insatiable curiosity about the out-of-doors. As a youth in Windsheim, a small village in Bavaria, he had spent endless fascinated hours in the Schossbach Forest, watching the blackcocks fighting in the spring, listening to the lonely mating call of the *auerhahn* like the tap of dripping rain, observing the colonies of plumed gray herons for which the forest was renowned. His father Jacob Stöller — the old family spelling — was a parish cantor, organist and singing master at the Church of St. Kilian; and young Georg Wilhelm's tenor voice, trained in his father's choir, earned him a scholarship at the University of Wittenberg to prepare for the Lutheran ministry. Flora and fauna proved more appealing than doctrines and dogma; and after a year he transferred to Halle University, where he studied botany and the closely allied science of medicine. In the anatomical theater he practiced surgery, operating on birds and mammals. A decade later on Bering Island his skill with the scalpel would enable him to dissect the great northern sea cow which bears his name today, and to write the only description of this now extinct species.

He graduated from Halle with highest honors, and was eligible for a chair in botany at his alma mater; but his eyes were fixed on more challenging horizons. All Europe was astir with news that the Empress Anna of Russia was mounting a vast expedition to extend her empire across the Pacific, the most ambitious voyage of discovery the world had yet known. The noted Danish explorer Vitus Bering would be in command, and several members of the Imperial Academy of Sciences at St. Petersburg would be invited to accompany him as far as Kamchatka. Steller was determined to be one of that select number. Unable to afford passage, he signed as medical adviser on a Russian army transport sailing home with invalided soldiers after the siege of Danzig; and in late November 1734, at the age of twenty-five, he landed in St. Petersburg with no money in his pocket, no friends to whom he could turn for help, nothing but his fierce and driving ambition.

The new Russian capital, which Peter the Great had founded thirty years before on a swampy delta of the Neva, was a pretentious and mongrel city of gilded radish-shaped domes and rococo Oriental palaces and gabled brick dwellings in the prim Holland style. They had been thrown together so hastily that roofs sagged and walls buckled, prompting an Italian visitor to remark tartly that "elsewhere ruins naturally become so, but in St. Petersburg they are built so." The population was about a hundred thousand, and as conglomerate as the architecture: Germans, French, Turks, Tatars, Kalmucks, Armenians, Bukharians. Social life centered around the Imperial Court, and was vulgar and decadent, only a step removed from the primitive. It was not unusual to meet "a Russian matron, dressed most gorgeously in damask and caparisoned with laces, but at the same time barefoot and carrying her slippers in her hand." Bewigged and perfumed noblemen and rouged ladies in imported Paris gowns rode in their scarlet troikas past the mutilated naked corpses of criminals, dangling on public display from gibbets along the main avenue. Over the metropolis lay the chill shadow of the gold-spired Fortress high above the Neva, where political offenders were knouted or beheaded, at the whim of the Empress, or consigned to the slave camps of Siberia.

Steller knew only a few words of Russian, and was bewildered by the babel of strange tongues. Ill at ease in the jostling and impersonal throng, he made his way across the river to the more congenial atmosphere of St. Petersburg's famed Apothecary Garden, a part of the naval hospital, where he wandered fascinated through the exotic hothouses, examining rare specimens which heretofore had been only names in a textbook. Here quite by chance he encountered the man who would play a vital role in shaping his career. The aging Archbishop Theophon of Novogorod, whose residence was close by, was taking his daily constitutional in the garden, and he noticed the slender blond youth engrossed in the botanical collections. Theophon paused to greet him in Russian and then, realizing that he was a foreigner, addressed him in Latin. Steller spoke Latin fluently, and they fell into easy conversation as they strolled together. The archbishop, himself a botanist of some reputation, was amazed at Steller's knowledge of the natural sciences and his precocious brilliance. His curiosity was aroused, and he plied him with questions: What was his background? Why had he come to this overcrowded city? Where was he staying?

Steller shrugged indifferently. Physical comforts never concerned him; he could go for days without food, and curl up in a doorway to sleep at night. "I have not made any arrangements."

The archbishop was turning over a thought in his mind. He had been ailing lately, and needed constant medical attention. Not only was Steller a doctor, but they shared the same scientific interests, and his gay and attractive personality could brighten a dull hour. "Would you care to live in the archiepiscopal palace as my resident physician and companion?"

Although he was Primate of the Russian Orthodox Church, Theophon was far from being a religious bigot, and was not averse to taking a Lutheran into his household. The members of his staff were allowed complete freedom, he possessed the best library in all Russia, and his cellar was famed for its malt and the fine beer brewed from it. He cut an awesome figure with his square white beard and flowing vestments and towering bishop's miter; but his smile was gentle and understanding, and his wise old eyes wrinkled with amusement at his protégé's proclivity for argument. Instead of being offended by Steller's brash manner, his dogmatic way of expressing himself, his intolerance when someone ventured to contradict him, Theophon made allowances for his Germanic bluntness and lack of tact. Behind the assertiveness, he knew, was a stubborn integrity, a belief in the truth of what he was saying; generally it turned out that he was right; and that made the archbishop a little sad. People may respect a man who is always right, but they love a man who is sometimes wrong. Theophon could foresee that all his life Steller would be disliked and lonely.

Steller could not have found a more influential patron. As the leading churchman of his time, Theophon had a dominant voice in both ecclesiastical and civic affairs. He had been an intimate friend of Peter the Great and had officiated at his funeral, and he enjoyed great prestige at the Imperial Court. When Steller confided his ambition to be admitted to the Academy of Sciences, a word from the archbishop was enough to obtain for him an appointment as Adjunct in Natural History, an assistant to the professorial staff. Now Steller's foot was planted on the first rung of the ladder. The next step was to be assigned to Bering's expedition and sent to Siberia and Kamchatka. Once there, he was certain that he could persuade Bering to take him on the voyage to America.

Virtually all scientific activity in St. Petersburg was confined to the ten-year-old Imperial Academy, which occupied an imposing edifice facing the Admiralty Palace across the Neva. The large proportion of its professoriat was made up of German intellectuals, imported by Peter the Great to enhance his country's prestige. They had formed an inner clique, speaking only German among themselves, and looked down on their Russian associates with smug superiority. It was inevitable that their arrogance should rub off on the young and impressionable adjunct, and he acquired a feeling of contempt for the Russians which was to cause much of his trouble later.

So sure was Steller that he would be ordered to Siberia that he made it his business to learn all he could of the country, and over the winter he visited frequently at the home of Dr. Daniel Messerschmidt, who had spent seven years exploring the Siberian wilderness. Dr. Messerschmidt was in his late fifties, moody and eccentric; the rigors of arctic travel had ruined his health, and he had fallen victim to a deep melancholia. He refused all offers of further employment when he returned to St. Petersburg, and lived in obscurity and abject poverty with his hot-blooded young wife Brigitte, whom acquaintances described as "a lively wild woman who was quite his opposite."

Brigitte was only a year older than Steller, of German peasant stock, big-boned and buxom and full of animal vitality. Her plump warm body was always moist with perspiration, and patches of damp powder were caked on her neck and between her breasts, brazenly revealed by a low-cut bodice. She was restless and unhappy with her morose husband; she had married him to gain social position and luxuries, and was bored by her cheerless existence. The attractive blond visitor offered a chance for the excitement she craved. While Steller pored over the Doctor's manuscripts of an evening, she would perch on the arm of the chair beside him, flirting with her eyes above the spread of her painted fan, smoothing his unruly hair with a heavily perfumed hand. Steller's unkempt appearance had an irresistible appeal for women. He never bothered with wig or powder, his rumpled long coat was unbuttoned, the pockets sagged with notebooks and botanical implements; and Brigitte was determined to possess and tame him. Steller was helpless to resist her seductive appeal, and for the first time in his life he found himself deeply in love. When Dr. Messerschmidt conveniently died the following spring, they talked of matrimony; but Steller could not support a wife on the meager salary of an adjunct, and it was decided to postpone their marriage until he obtained a more lucrative assignment with Bering's expedition. "Then will you travel with me to Siberia?"

"I'll follow you wherever you go," Brigitte pledged.

Bering had left St. Petersburg in 1733, the year before Steller's arrival, and was progressing with glacial slowness across the five thousand mile expanse of Russia and Siberia toward the Pacific. Wagons still rumbled eastward with added supplies from the Admiralty storehouse to support the huge army of shipbuilders, carpenters, blacksmiths, cooks, servants, sailors. The French astronomer Louis de la Croyere, a member of the Academy, had already been selected to sail with Bering, and two other professors, Gerhard Friedrich Müller and Johann Georg Gmelin, were moving across Siberia with the expedition, gathering plants and seeds and native artifacts. Steller was beside himself with frustration as crates of specimens arrived in St. Petersburg from faroff rivers with magic names: the Ob, the Irtysh, the Lena.

His chance came in 1736, when Bering was two-thirds of the way across Siberia. Müller and Gmelin had been complaining of overwork, and the Academy decided to send another scientist to assist them. Again the influential Archbishop Theophon intervened on behalf of his protégé, and on his recommendation the Imperial Senate assigned Adjunct Steller as field biologist in Kamchatka. His joy at the news was tempered by the sudden death, early in September, of his great benefactor. With the passing of Theophon, Steller lost the only friend who ever understood him.

Now he had an established position and a guaranteed salary of six hundred rubles a year; and at last Steller was able to wed Dr. Messerschmidt's widow "in a public assembly with the usual ceremonies." Though Brigitte had promised to accompany Steller on his journey and share his hardships, it developed on their honeymoon that she was interested only in sharing his income. There was a violent quarrel, but Mrs. Steller had had enough of frugal living and refused to leave St. Petersburg. Steller made a settlement of the furnishings he had purchased for their future home and two hundred rubles a year, and set out alone for Siberia, disillusioned and bitter. Brigitte promptly sold the furniture and embarked on a gay whirl in the gambling parlors of the dissolute capital. It was the last time Steller ever saw her.

The bitterness left its mark. Steller's whole personality changed, and he became more irascible, short-tempered, opinionated and dogmatic. His tongue grew sharp and biting, his sensitive mouth yanked down at the corners in a smile that had no mirth. In an effort to put Brigitte out of his mind, he immersed himself in his scientific work as he crossed the monotonous steppes, finding a substitute interest in the strange plants and birds of eastern Siberia. Two years after his unfortunate marriage, he was able to assure Gmelin: "My wife is much too brazen, and recently demanded perforce 400 rubles at once because she fancies that in Siberia straw is cheap and snow melts on the tongue . . . I have in her stead two young ravens." He concluded: "I have quite forgotten her and fallen in love with Nature, *nam cessante causa cessat effectus* [for if the cause ceases, the effect ceases also]."

He caught up with Gmelin and Müller early in January of 1739. His fellow scientists were moving across Siberia in royal style with a caravan of cooks and servants, secretaries and artists, surveyors and soldiers, drivers and horses by the score to transport their library of several hundred reference books and their special wines and table delicacies. They were aghast at Steller's spartan method of travel. "As it is necessary in Siberia to carry along one's own housekeeping outfit," Gmelin observed in amazement, "he had reduced it to the least possible compass. His drinking cup for beer was the same as his cup for mead and whiskey. Wine he dispensed with entirely. He had only one dish out of which he ate and in which was served all his food. For this he needed no chef. He cooked everything himself and that with so little circumstance that soup, vegetables and meat were put into the same pot and boiled together."

They were overjoyed to see their young assistant. Müller was in poor health and planned to return to St. Petersburg; Gmelin himself was weary of constant haggling with the naval and civic authorities, and had petitioned to be recalled. In Steller they found a man who was able and even eager to relieve them of their burdensome duties. Gmelin described him as "exceedingly exact and so indefatigable that . . . we need not have the slightest anxiety. It was no hardship for him to go hungry and thirsty a whole day if he was able to accomplish something advantageous to science. No matter how vividly we depicted the privations, such representations acted only as a stronger incentive." To their relief, and Steller's private delight, he was left with their servants and equipage to carry on alone the "description of the natural history of Kamchatka as Her Imperial Majesty's order required and the wise arrangements of the Academy of Sciences demanded." Now there would be no rival naturalist to share in his discoveries. All that remained was to secure a berth on Bering's ship.

There was no time to be lost. Bering was already at Okhotsk, the easternmost Siberian port opposite Kamchatka, where the two vessels he was building to carry his expedition across the Pacific were nearing completion. As soon as the weather moderated, Steller set out on the final leg of his arduous journey, beset by irritating delays. Rivers could not be navigated until the ice was out. Living quarters were already commandeered by naval personnel, and he had to write his scientific reports in windowless and smoke-filled native huts. Local bureaucrats blocked him at every turn, and he made no effort to hide his fury at these ignorant petty officials. When he was refused boats for transportation, he built his own barge and sculled his supplies six hundred miles down the Lena. It was not until May of 1740 that he reached Yakutsk, where Bering had spent three heartbreaking years, and engaged a team of small hairy Siberian horses to haul his party over the wild Yablonni Mountains to Okhotsk.

On the trail he was overtaken by Captain Martin Spanberg, who had led an expedition to the Kurile Islands and Japan the previous summer. Malicious letters from enemies in Siberia had hinted to the Imperial Senate that the captain's claims were false, that he had visited Korea and not Japan. Senatorial suspicions were aroused, and Spanberg, on his way home to St. Petersburg in triumph, had been met by a courier with orders to return to Okhotsk and repeat his former voyage. He was in great haste to reach the port before Bering sailed for Kamchatka, in order to obtain a vessel for his second expedition; and Steller left his party, with instructions to follow as rapidly as possible, and galloped with Spanberg down the Ural River valley.

Captain Spanberg was a Dane like Bering, a good practical mariner but without culture, overbearing and tyrannical to his underlings. His reputation for wilfulness and cruelty had spread all over Siberia, and the inhabitants regarded him as a "runaway galley-slave" whose brutality was matched only by his greed for gain. He was usually accompanied by a huge dog which, the legend went, he would set upon anyone who offended him. He was given to loud bragging of his exploits, and Steller listened in fascination as the captain described the natives of the Kuriles who had not "even retained the full appearance of human beings. They were everywhere overgrown with hair, like bears, with this difference, however, that on their neck down towards the back the hair was much longer, resembling in every way a horse's mane." Steller set down the words in his journal, the first description of the Hairy Ainu tribesmen who had formerly inhabited Japan. His imagination caught fire; if Bering refused him passage, he thought, he might do worse than to accompany Spanberg on his voyage.

Bering's two new vessels, named for the apostles St. Peter and St. Paul, had left the stocks and were riding at anchor when Steller and Spanberg arrived at Okhotsk on August 12, 1740. The ships, built in the style of the packet boats which plied the Baltic, were identical in size and design, each 80 feet long and 22 feet in beam, with a 9½ foot draught. They were rigged as brigs and armed with fourteen guns, two and three pounders. Since no food except fish could be obtained in Kamchatka, Bering had borrowed the double-sloop *Nadezhda*, one of the ships used by Spanberg on his first Japan expedition, and the small government-owned galiot *Okhotsk* to transport provisions and supplies to Avacha Bay, from which the *St. Peter* and *St. Paul* would sail the following spring. He planned to leave Okhotsk on the fifteenth, and the supply ships were fully loaded and ready for departure.

Spanberg's abrupt return caught the Captain Commander completely by surprise. Despite the official orders from the Senate, he refused to unload the *Nadezhda* and turn it back to Spanberg. His own expedition had already consumed seven years and enormous sums of money, and he was being harassed by humiliating dispatches from St. Petersburg urging him to waste no more time and get under way at once. He explained patiently that the American voyage was the prime object of the whole immense enterprise, and Spanberg would have to build another vessel. Spanberg pointed out that this might delay his trip as much as a year, but Bering was adamant, and the junior captain ranted and threatened in vain. Steller, who was present at the stormy interview, wrote that Spanberg conducted himself "in such a manner that, while it might be said he was a captain, nevertheless he had not forgotten the lowest tricks of a sailor."

It was the first meeting between Steller and Captain Commander Bering, and there was an immediate sympathy between them, though they were opposites in almost every way. Bering was fifty-nine, a huge kindly man with a round moon of a face and placid sea-blue eyes. He had the Danish qualities of stolidity, lack of any visible emotion, a taciturn moodiness which made him seem remote and unapproachable. He walked with a slight stoop, as though his responsibilities rested heavily on him, and of late he had become increasingly slow-spoken and deliberate, weighing every possible consequence before taking action. Like the Archbishop Theophon, he was instantly drawn to the ingratiating young naturalist, and impressed by his medical knowledge and his sharp incisive mind; but all Steller's charm failed to elicit an invitation from the cautious Captain Commander. "I have no orders to take you along, Mr. Steller, nor have you any authorization to proceed further than Kamchatka."

"But my work on the expedition would be in line with my assigned duties," Steller pleaded. "I am sure the Academy would not want such an opportunity to be wasted."

Bering shook his head wearily. "I do not wish any further trouble with St. Petersburg. The best I can offer you is passage on the *Nadezhda* across the Sea of Okhotsk to Bolsheretsk."

Steller left the interview in dark dejection. His dream of

discovering the new continent was shattered. That night he
dispatched an unhappy letter to the Senate, requesting permission to accompany Captain Spanberg to Japan.

At Okhotsk Steller shared quarters with his ranking colleague at the Academy, Louis de la Croyere, who had arrived
earlier in the summer with nine wagonloads of equipment.
The French astronomer was short and compact in build, a
vain and fussy and foppish martinet. His pompous manner reminded Steller of a pouter pigeon, ruffling out his feathers in
self-importance, walking daintily with his toes touching the
ground first. He had a habit of ducking his head up and down
for emphasis when he talked, like a pigeon pecking corn. Even
in their crude surroundings, he was elegantly dressed in the
latest Paris fashion: an embroidered silk waistcoat partly unbuttoned to show his frilled shirt, flaring cuffs heavy with
gold thread, long lace fringes at his wrists. He affected low
pumps with jeweled buckles, and his white stockings were
padded with false calves to give shape to his spindly legs. His
wig was carefully curled and powdered blue, and he regarded
Steller's casual attire disapprovingly through a lorgnette with
a single eyeglass. In the midst of a conversation together, he
would pause to sprinkle snuff along the back of his hand,
breathe it in with a loud sniff, and sneeze into his lace handkerchief, which he had drenched with perfume to offset the
offensive odor of his companion's native-tanned jacket and
sealskin boots.

De la Croyere's commission from the Academy placed him
"in charge of the astronomical, physical and other scientific
observations of that nature." He had obtained the appointment
only through the prestige of his illustrious half brother, the
noted geographer Joseph Nicolas Delisle; his actual knowledge of astronomy was as elementary as his instruments.

After a rough trip down the Lena, he had written Gmelin requesting the services of a man capable of adjusting his seventeen pendulum clocks, by which he made all his calculations. Gmelin located a former clockmaker who had been exiled to Siberia for a sex offense, and de la Croyere engaged him as his personal repairman. Both Gmelin and Müller were well aware of his addiction to gambling and drinking, and Steller, having come home night after night to discover his fellow academician in a sodden stupor, wrote Gmelin in disgust: "He is morally worn out . . . so deep in debt that he does not know which way to turn; his instruments are unfit for observations." Even the easygoing and tolerant Bering had no liking for de la Croyere, but refrained from dismissing him for fear that it might provoke another argument with St. Petersburg.

Bering's scheduled departure on the fifteenth was delayed by a last-minute dispatch from the Senate, requesting the Captain Commander to submit an exhaustive report on his future plans. To save time, he ordered the *Nadezhda* to proceed as far as Bolsheretsk, carrying a cargo of precious foodstuffs including the expedition's two-year supply of biscuits baked at Yakutsk. The skipper of the sloop was Fleet Master Sofron Khitrov, a boastful and surly officer in the Royal Navy. Though Khitrov claimed that he was an experienced navigator, Bering had never seen him handle a ship; but the Captain Commander was hard pressed and decided to entrust him with the command. De la Croyere brought aboard his pendulum clocks and telescopes and ubiquitous repairman, nicknamed the Immoral Clockmaker; Steller followed him over the rail, carrying all his belongings in a canvas bag slung across a shoulder; and the *Nadezhda* weighed anchor and started down the Okhota River.

Khitrov gripped the wheel with shaggy black fists, staring at the water and ignoring his passengers. He was thickset and squat, and his solid shoulders, slanting down from a bull neck, seemed to strain at his faded blue naval jacket. His face had been battered in youthful waterfront brawls, the nose was flattened, and a thickened ridge of cartilage on his forehead almost hid his gray eyes, as hard as pebbles. When he was angry, his voice rose to a high hoarse whisper, and his lips struggled to form words. Brute strength was his only standard in judging a man, and he regarded the mincing and effeminate de la Croyere and the slightly built Steller as beneath his notice. He had not even acknowledged their greeting when they boarded the sloop.

Steller, standing in the bow as they approached the broad delta at the river's mouth, saw a half-exposed sandbar dead ahead, and the main current cutting sharply to the right. He shouted a warning, but Khitrov did not deign to heed him. A moment later the sloop ran aground with a heavy jolt and the tortured groan of spreading timbers. Water poured through the damaged sides, and de la Croyere, with a birdlike chirp of distress, fluttered down into the hold and emerged clutching an armload of dripping clocks. Steller had no patience with stupidity, and his short temper exploded in a series of Russian and German invectives. "*Dura! Dummkopf!*" he shouted at the Fleet Master. "Did you learn to navigate on the Siberian steppes?" Khitrov made no reply, but his tiny pebble eyes were malevolent.

Another couple of weeks were wasted while the *Nadezhda* was towed back to Okhotsk to be patched and refloated; but Khitrov's mishap had an even more disastrous result. Because of the shortness of the Arctic summer, Bering had planned to spend two years on the voyage, and carry sufficient foodstuffs to winter in America. Now he was forced to make a fateful change in his plan. The sea biscuits, ruined by salt water, were irreplaceable; because of their loss, he would have to sail to America and back in a single summer.

It was not until September 21 that the little fleet of four vessels reached the mouth of Bolshaya Reka, the Great River, on the west coast of Kamchatka, a dreary shoreline of sand dunes and brackish swamps. Steller and de la Croyere transferred to the little galiot *Okhotsk* and proceeded upstream to the inland port of Bolsheretsk, where the French astronomer had elected to spend the fall until accommodations could be prepared at Avacha Bay; and Bering's three other ships sailed at once to reach the harbor on the Pacific side before freezeup. Again the luckless Khitrov bungled in his navigation. As he tried to round Cape Lopatka, the southern tip of the peninsula, the *Nadezhda* struck a reef and had to limp back ignominiously to Bolsheretsk, where its cargo was unloaded to be transported overland during the winter. Steller could not resist a pointed salutation: "Well done, Fleet Master Khitrov. You have demonstrated your seamanship again."

The barb sank deep, and Khitrov's bull neck swelled and he took a step forward, fists knotted. His lips worked soundlessly, unable to frame an answer, and he swung on his heel and stalked away.

Bolsheretsk was a bleak collection of wooden huts gathered around the *ostrog*, a log stockade which enclosed the government quarters. In all there were some thirty buildings, including a public house and a vodka distillery. As in most remote settlements, the civil authorities were corrupt, and residents were subjected to every kind of extortion. The governor of Kamchatka enriched himself by bribes; the naval personnel at the fort exacted tribute with the cat-o'-nine-tails; even the forty-six cossack soldiers in the garrison had to pay a head-tax. The residents in turn exploited the more primitive Kamchadals in the surrounding country, charging exorbitant prices for merchandise and compelling the tribes to reimburse them in furs, which they sold at great profit. Steller was outraged by the immorality and avarice of the Russian officials and the condition of the oppressed natives, and determined to make formal complaint to the Imperial Senate.

De la Croyere established himself in comfortable rooms at the public house, handy to the distillery, and assembled his seventeen pendulum clocks to observe the coming eclipse of Jupiter's first satellite. Steller's restless energy would not allow him to remain idle. A student from the Academy of Sciences, Stepan Krasheninnikov, had been doing some preliminary exploration on the peninsula, and Steller wrote him a peremptory letter: "You are under my orders and must make a report to me of everything you have done and observed from your arrival in Kamchatka to this time." Krasheninnikov was obsequious and deferential to his superior, but he resented Steller's officious manner. During the waning autumn months, they embarked on a study of the fishes and crustaceans in the numerous streams and rivers, and Steller described for the first time the life cycle of the anadromous North Pacific salmon — how it comes in from the sea to spawn in fresh water and die — and identified its five species by the names still in use today: *gorbuscha*, humpback; *keta*, chum; *nerka*, red or sockeye; *kisutch*, silver; and *tshawytscha*, king. Following Steller's death, Krasheninnikov published the discoveries under his own signature in his *Kamchatkan Observations*.

Shortly after Christmas, de la Croyere and his retinue set out in grand style to cross the peninsula to Avacha Bay; and Steller watched his departure with a heavy heart. It did not seem right that this pompous and incompetent academician should be privileged to sail to America, while Steller had to forego the coveted opportunity and remain behind, with only the faint hope of accompanying Spanberg to Japan next year. To forget his disappointment, he borrowed the young *slushiv* Lepekhin in January and journeyed south through precipitous mountain country as far as Cape Lopatka, returning to Bolsheretsk toward the end of February. The dispatch from Bering was awaiting him when he arrived.

Avacha Bay is one of the world's finest harbors, a round basin eleven miles in diameter with a uniform depth of twelve fathoms, sheltered from ocean storms by a bottleneck entrance. To the north three active volcanoes rise like ramparts to 11,000 feet, and a perpetual plume of smoke from the highest peak veers with the wind like a weathervane. Natural breakwaters divide the bay into several smaller harbors; and the innermost, doubly protected by a high wooded peninsula and a narrow gravel spit, had been selected as expedition headquarters.

The *St. Peter* and the *St. Paul*, unrigged and made secure for the winter, were locked in the ice that still covered Avacha Bay. Behind them, on a height of land overlooking the harbor, stood a miniature village of log houses which Bering had christened Petropavlovsk, after his two vessels. The Captain Commander and his ranking officers occupied a long oblong structure in the center; at the water's edge was the *magazin* or storage shed; the barracks of the petty officers and men were on the opposite side of the harbor, adjoining the sod huts of some Kamchadals who had been hired for construction work. A deeply religious man, Bering had erected a small church near his quarters, called the Chapel of St. Peter and St. Paul.

The room of the Captain Commander was in a corner of the headquarters building, separated by a partition from the main dormitory. It was no more than a windowless closet, barely large enough to contain his cot and chair and crude plank table. The table was spread with maps and charts, and Bering was bent over them, trying to plot the course of his voyage by the light of a guttering candle.

It was a hopeless task. The maps were vague and conflicting, based on supposition and rumor, and no two were alike. Some cartographers indicated a large land mass southeast of Kamchatka, reported by the early explorer Juan de Gama and known as Gama Land. Other charts showed a mysterious island called Yezo, said to be rich in silver and gold, lying about four hundred miles east of Japan. The French geographer Delisle portrayed both Yezo and Gama Land as part of Asia, and Japan as a peninsula attached to the mainland. On only one point did the maps agree: the west coast of America ended with the Spanish discoveries in California, and north of the 38th parallel every chart was blank. No one knew the shape or size of the remaining American continent. No one could say whether Bolshaya Zemlya was part of Asia or of America, or indeed whether it even existed. No one was sure whether the upper section of the map, labeled North Pacific, was partly land or all water.

The maps and charts began to swim before him, and Bering leaned back and passed a weary hand across his eyes. He had been aware for some months that his health was failing. In January his chief surgeon had declined to make the voyage, and requested to be sent back to St. Petersburg. Bering needed a doctor aboard, and he recalled the likable naturalist and physician he had left at the Bolshaya River. He had another and more personal motive in sending for Steller. Despite his years of loyal service in the Imperial Navy, he was still regarded as a foreigner. With the young German at his side, he would not feel so much alone among his jealous Russian associates.

There was a knock on the door, and he rose as Steller entered, and held out his hand. Their greeting was perfunctory; Bering had a Danish aversion to showing his emotions, but Steller knew that the older man was profoundly moved to see him. He seated himself on an empty nail keg, the only other item of furniture in the room, and Bering filled his pipe and lit it from the candle before he spoke. Steller noticed that the flame shook in his unsteady hand.

He peered at the Captain Commander more closely in the candlelight, shocked at the change which had come over him in the few months since their interview at Okhotsk. The facial muscles had slackened, and the fleshy cheeks and jowls sagged in folds, giving him a drawn and haggard look. His grizzled hair had turned white as any wig, and his once powerful voice was a hollow echo, as though the strain of the past years had drained him of all vitality. The words came slowly, with long pauses between them. "Mr. Steller, it is my desire that you accompany me on the voyage to America."

Steller sought to conceal his eagerness. It was clear that the Captain Commander was as anxious to have him as he was to join the expedition. Their previous roles were reversed; now it was Bering who was asking a favor, and Steller's quick mind saw the opportunity to lay down certain conditions. He affected an air of indecision. "There are difficulties, your Excellency. Since coming to Kamchatka, I have begun to realize the vast amount of work before me. Much as I desire to accept your offer, I should incur the displeasure of the Academy, and possibly suffer severe punishment, if I were to disregard instructions and quit my assignment before it was completed."

"But the work required on the expedition would be precisely in line with your duties," Bering pleaded, unconsciously echoing Steller's own argument. "Let me write the Academy and assure them that it would be an unforgivable mistake to let such an opportunity slip by."

Still Steller appeared to hesitate. "I have another problem, sir. I have already petitioned the Governing Senate for permission to join Captain Spanberg's expedition to Japan next summer. What if this permission should arrive while I was in America?"

"I am supreme commander of the Kamchatka Expedition, Mr. Steller." For a moment, Bering's eyes showed their former fire. "I'll take the whole responsibility upon myself, and be answerable for any consequences."

"I'm afraid it would be impossible for me to undertake the work singlehanded."

Bering brushed aside his objection. "There'll be a draftsman aboard, Frederic Plenisner, who will be assigned to you as artist, and the assistant surgeon Betge will be at your disposal."

"I'd also need a hunter, sir. My *slushiv* Lepekhin is an excellent shot."

"He can sign with the crew."

Steller had one more point to settle. In the Russian navy, he knew, it was obligatory for the commanding officer to consult a *soviet* of all his officers, and abide by their decision. "I have reason to believe that Master Khitrov would not welcome me aboard."

"I'll call a ship's council and have your assignment approved by each officer in writing." Bering seemed to be fighting an overpowering fatigue, and his voice lowered. "I am not a well man, Mr. Steller," he confided. "It would be a comfort to have someone with your medical knowledge in case . . ." He did not finish the sentence. "Will you come?"

Steller nodded, satisfied, and they shook hands again and

he departed. Bering stood staring at the closed door for a moment, laid his pipe on the table, and stretched out on his cot, the back of a hand resting over his eyes. He was exhausted in body and spirit. All he wanted was to see the expedition launched and on its way. Then at last he could rest.

II. THE CAPTAIN COMMANDER

V ITUS JONASSEN BERING was born in 1681 in the sea-coast town of Horsens in Denmark. He came of pious stock, descended from a long line of Lutheran clergymen, and had planned as a boy to enter the ministry; but his father was too poor to support the large family of children, and in order to relieve pressure at home young Bering shipped to sea. In his early twenties he joined the newly organized Russian navy as a sublieutenant. He proved to be a competent officer, dependable and considerate of the men under him, and was promoted to captain second rank as a reward for his skillful handling of transport operations during the Swedish War. His success attracted the attention of Peter the Great; and when the Emperor decided to send an expedition to explore the North Pacific, Bering was promoted to captain first rank and placed in command.

Peter had long been curious to determine how far the confines of his empire extended to the east. There were vague rumors of a strait between the old and new worlds, and Bering was ordered to sail north from Kamchatka and determine whether or not the continents of Asia and America were joined. He was assigned two lieutenants: Martin Spanberg, his fellow countryman, and a capable but calculating Russian named Alexei Chirikov. In 1725 Bering's First Kamchatka Expedition sailed north from the mouth of the Kamchatka River, through the straits which bear his name today, as far as Siberia's East Cape. Here his overriding sense of caution halted him. Fearing that his vessel would be trapped and crushed in the ice, he turned back without rounding the cape and thus failed to settle the question of Russia's link with America. On his return voyage he passed an island, previously hidden by fog, which he named St. Diomede, now Big Diomede. Chirikov urged him to investigate it further; but they were in strange waters, with winter closing in, and he refused to veer off course. Had he circumnavigated the island, he might have seen the coast of Alaska, only twenty-five miles away.

Bering knew in his heart why he had failed. He was a sailor, not an explorer. He lacked the spirit of bold and reckless adventure; he was bred in the tradition that a skipper's first duty is to bring his ship safely home. When he returned to St. Petersburg after the voyage, his discoveries were held to be inconclusive, and he was publicly discredited. Anxious to vindicate himself, he requested the Empress Anna, successor to Peter, to give him another chance; and in the spring of 1731 — just ten years ago — he was given the rank of captain commander and placed in charge of the Second Kamchatka Expedition. Chirikov, promoted to captain, served again as his next in command.

The past ten years had been a nightmare. Although originally conceived as a voyage of discovery, the enterprise had grown more and more unwieldly as further duties were imposed on Bering. The Imperial Senate ordered him to open up all of northeastern Asia, to introduce cattle-raising on the Pacific coast, to found schools for elementary and nautical instruction. He was to establish shipyards and ropewalks for the construction of his vessels, iron mines and foundries to turn out chains and anchors, lighthouses and storage depots and even a bimonthly postal communication service from St. Petersburg to Kamchatka and down to the border of China.

The Admiralty added its own requirements to his mounting burden. Not only was the entire Asian coast to be charted, but he was instructed to map the shoreline of America as far south as California, survey the Kurile Islands and Japan, and explore the Ob and the Lena rivers north to the Arctic Ocean. The Academy of Sciences handicapped him further by sending along a small cavalcade of professors and their assistants to conduct a complete scientific and geodetic investigation of all Siberia and Kamchatka, including its natural history and the ethnology of its native tribes. From a modest beginning, the personnel had multiplied to several thousand men and servants, a disorganized and cumbersome army.

Memories of their journey still came back at night to torment him. They had started from St. Petersburg in 1733 on the long trek across Russia and Siberia to the Pacific, almost a third of the distance around the globe. Much of Siberia rests on permafrost, covered with snow for nine months and a desolate wasteland of swamps and soggy tundra the rest of the year. Cannon sank out of sight in the quaking moss. Horses slipped and fell through the ice, and had to be abandoned. Swarms of mosquitoes and black flies and midges covered the faces and hands of the men in summer, and were drawn down into the throat with each breath. River beds were filled with rocks and trunks of fallen trees, and boatmen walked the slippery banks and hauled their clumsy flat-bottomed barges over the snags. In places where the current was too strong, thirty men would wade up to their waists in the rapids and carry the barge on their shoulders. The icy water was cauterizing, and their legs were soon covered with boils and festering sores. During the day the heat was oppressive, but nights were bitter cold, and the sweat-soaked clothing froze on their bodies. Many failed to stir in the morning, and their corpses were left to the packs of wolves which howled constantly in the expedition's wake.

Game was scarce and habitations were few and far between; in a stretch of a thousand miles they found only one Russian hut. Food was seized from the nomad tribes, under threat of the knout. Convict laborers borrowed from Siberian prison camps tried to desert, and were hanged from gallows that lined the trail. Local civic authorities resented the ravenous horde who descended on their settlements, plundering their meager supply of rations and vodka and spreading disease among their women, and they refused Bering any cooperation. His own conniving officers wrote letters home containing slanderous gossip about the Captain Commander, and St. Petersburg buzzed with rumors that Bering was carrying on a contraband liquor trade, that he was lining his pockets through embezzlement of government funds, that he had abducted a group of native girls in Yakutsk for his personal harem.

The Empress Anna grew more and more impatient as the years dragged on and expenses mounted. The Academy of Sciences, which had always been hostile to Bering, took pains to point out that he had originally estimated the cost of the enterprise at twelve thousand rubles, whereas the figure had already exceeded three hundred thousand rubles and he was only two-thirds of the way to the Pacific. The Empress ordered the Admiralty College to see if the Second Kamchatka Expedition "can be brought to a head, so that the treasury shall not be emptied in vain." The Admiralty, seeking a scapegoat, put the entire blame on Bering, threatened him with court-martial, and cut his pay in half from 1737 until late in 1740.

His energy and initiative were spent by the time he reached Avacha Bay that fall; but his troubles were not over. Khitrov's loss of their winter provisions in the Okhota River faced him with the terrible urgency of confining his voyage to one summer. The Fleet Master's second accident off Cape Lopatka, and his return to Bolsheretsk, proved to be an even greater calamity. There were no horses in Kamchatka, and all the supplies from the damaged *Nadezhda* had to be freighted to Avacha Bay by dogsled or on the backs of natives, a difficult and time-consuming undertaking. Since there was not sufficient manpower in Bolsheretsk, tribesmen from the surrounding countryside were impressed into service, some seized from homes as much as three hundred miles distant.

The fierce Koryals rebelled at their conscription, and the more docile Kamchadals followed suit. The mutiny spread, seven Russians were slain, and armed troops had to be dispatched from Bolsheretsk to quell the revolt. The Russian method of forcing the natives into submission was to surprise some women and children in an underground shelter, light the fuse of a hand grenade, and drop it through the smokehole in the roof. Bering's first officer, Lieutenant Sven Waxell, who had been sent to supervise the transportation, wrote: "When a grenade fell among them, they . . . ran forward to look at it, laughing and wondering what on earth it could be. In the end the grenade exploded, wounding many and killing several." The insurrection was suppressed, but not before several valuable months had been wasted. It was time that Bering could ill afford to lose.

Upon his arrival at Avacha Bay, Steller moved into the east wing of the headquarters building, again sharing quarters with de la Croyere. The fastidious little academician showed no great pleasure at their reunion. His nose wrinkled at the ripe aroma of sweat-stained leather and seal oil, and he reached for his snuffbox and scented handkerchief. He made no secret of his loathing for the primitive living conditions at Petropavlovsk, avoided the company of his coarse associates, and spent all his time in his room playing cards with the Immoral Clockmaker and saturating himself with vodka.

Steller could not be idle. The deep snow precluded any exploring around Avacha Bay, and his pent-up energy needed some outlet. He had been brooding about the mistreatment of the natives at Bolsheretsk, and with a crusading sense of public duty he composed a series of intemperate letters to St. Petersburg, criticizing the local government and making suggestions for its improvement. He informed the Holy Synod of the deplorable state of the clergy, and urged that missionaries be sent to Kamchatka, not only to convert and baptize the natives, but also to attend to the obvious spiritual needs of the corrupt Russian officials. In his supreme self-assurance, he went into the military situation, and listed several new sites to build palisaded forts. Gmelin, who saw the correspondence, observed wryly to his colleague Müller: "The most laughable part of it is that he recommended places for the establishment of *ostrogs* where on account of the lack of timber it would be impossible to build. No one dares to be so bold as to contradict him, for in that case he would at once incur the ill-luck of being persecuted by him."

Not content with antagonizing the Senate, Steller dispatched indiscreet protests to both the Admiralty College and the Academy of Sciences, though he was prudent enough to reverse the addresses. To the Admiralty he complained that the Academy was represented by incompetent scientists such as de la Croyere, whose abysmal ignorance jeopardized the whole expedition. To the Academy he wrote that the medical kit which the Admiralty had supplied for the voyage contained no antiscorbutics for warding off scurvy. He was right on both counts; but his advice was unsolicited and considered presumptuous, and the letters were ignored.

With the approach of spring breakup, Captain Commander Bering prepared the final crew roster. The personnel were divided almost evenly between the two vessels: seventy-seven on the *St. Peter* and seventy-six on the *St. Paul*. Bering decided to sail on the former, and his second in command, Captain Chirikov, was assigned to the sister ship. Lieutenant Waxell was made Bering's first officer, and Fleet Master Khitrov was selected as his second lieutenant, partly because Bering wanted to keep a close eye on him after his previous unfortunate experiences, and partly because he felt it would be tactful to have at least one Russian among his ranking officers. Andreyan Hesselberg, an experienced old pilot, was first mate; Frederic Plenisner was draftsman and "conductor"; and Steller was listed as mineralogist, with Thoma Lepekhin as his servant. Bering carefully arranged for de la Croyere to travel on the *St. Paul* with Chirikov, accompanied by his repairman. It turned out that the Immoral Clockmaker had no intention of taking part in the great adventure; de la Croyere's pleas were of no avail, and he was left behind in Petropavlovsk.

Khitrov had been assigned to keep the ship's log, and his first entry was on April 23, 1741, when work was started on rerigging and loading the vessels. Delayed supplies were still trickling into Petropavlovsk by dogsled, but Bering was anxious to be on his way as soon as the harbor ice went out. On May 4, during a violent snowstorm, he called a *soviet* of all the officers and men to decide on the course which would be followed to America. Steller was not invited to the council, but de la Croyere was present in powdered wig and gleaming silks and satins, as exotic as a parrot in the dark swarthy company. He had brought a copy of the map drawn by his half-brother Delisle, and his head ducked up and down as he spoke with a complacent air of authority. "I do not need to remind the Captain Commander that he has been instructed to search first for the territory called Gama Land."

Bering hesitated, fumbling and irresolute. Privately he had no confidence in the Delisle map. Steller had protested vehemently that the territory existed only on paper, and insisted that he "could prove with more than twenty conclusive reasons where the land is nearest." Furthermore, Bering recalled, Spanberg had sailed over the same section of ocean last year and found nothing. His own better judgment was against wasting any of the short summer months in a fruitless search, but he was unwilling to challenge the cocksure little academician, and attempted a weak compromise. "Perhaps we could sail direct to America and explore for Gama Land on our return in the fall."

De la Croyere inhaled a pinch of snuff, and sneezed delicately. His polite French voice was edged. "That would be contrary to your orders, Commander," he reminded him.

Reluctantly Bering yielded, and the council agreed to lay their course SE by E as far as the 46th parallel. If Gama Land had not been sighted by then, they would alter course to E by NE. Had they ignored the fabrications of Delisle and sailed due east at the start of their voyage, Lieutenant Waxell wrote, "we should have reached the American mainland in eight days." In his memoirs of the expedition, set down over a decade afterward, Waxell was still bitter about the Academy's "unfounded and false" map which cost so many lives. "I know I am writing all too much of this matter, but I can hardly

tear myself away from it, for my blood still boils whenever I
think of the scandalous deception of which we were the victims."

Spring was unusually late that year. Khitrov's log on May
1 reported that the ice was still so thick around the vessels
that it was necessary to chop a hole to let the small bow anchor
into the water. Gradually the snow receded, bare patches of
ground appeared, and the migratory birds returned to Avacha Bay. Steller made use of his spare time, while the ships
were being loaded, to study the wildlife of the area. He identified the wagtail and also the magpie, which he remembered
seeing as a boy in Windsheim, and recorded them in his lost
manuscript on the birds of Kamchatka. Among the fishes in
the bay, he dissected and described the green-fleshed rock
trout, a hitherto unknown species in Asia, which was later
named *Hexagrammos stelleri*, Steller's Greenling.

By May 22 the ships were sufficiently readied for the
crews to bring their bags aboard and occupy their quarters.
Khitrov noted spitefully in his log that a sailor "took out from
one of the casks on board a bucket of vodka and gave it to
Adjunct Steller. We . . . made a bed for Adjunct Steller in
the Commander's cabin." On Sunday, May 24, Bering hoisted
his flag on the *St. Peter* and made a final inspection of both
crews prior to departure. As they were about to hoist sail, the
wind failed them, and four days were lost while they lay in a
dead calm. Early in the morning of the twenty-ninth a slight
breeze stirred, and Bering ordered a gun fired as a signal for
church services to invoke divine blessing. The breeze dropped
off as suddenly as it had come, and the vessels had to be rowed
out of the inner harbor and anchored in the open roadstead,
waiting for a prosperous wind.

Three more days went by while the crews warped the ships

toward the mouth of Avacha Bay, and Bering chafed at the added delay. On the evening of June second, a sloop was sighted outside, making for the entrance. It was the ill-fated *Nadezhda*, bringing the rest of the supplies which could not be transported overland. Her arrival was too late to be of any benefit to the expedition, and she sailed into the inner harbor and discharged her cargo ashore.

Early in the afternoon of June 4 the wind steadied from the northwest. The two vessels made sail and steered through the narrow mouth of the bay. The channel lay between the jagged pinnacles called the Three Brothers and the sheer side of Babushkin Rock. Myriad flocks of gulls and kittiwakes and cormorants, disturbed on their nests along the ledges, set up a deafening raucous protest. "Carrying all sails except the spritsail," they cut twin furrows eastward, and Khitrov began his reckoning from the landmark called Vaua at the harbor entrance, where Bering had built a lighthouse.

Slowly the coastline disappeared below the horizon, until the three volcanoes seemed to float on the sea. The Captain Commander stood on the afterdeck, gazing in silence at the receding land. Perhaps he knew then that he would not see it again. He turned over the command to Waxell, and retired to his cabin.

III. VOYAGE TO THE UNKNOWN

FOR SEVERAL DAYS the weather held clear and cold, with a topgallantsail wind blowing briskly out of the northwest. Occasional scud clouds crossed the sun, trailing their shadows over the level ocean, and the long even swells rose and fell as regularly as breathing. The *St. Peter* and the *St. Paul* set their course SE by E, as decided at the ship's council in Petropavlovsk, and lookouts in the crosstrees scanned the horizon for any sign of the chimerical Gama Land which Delisle had depicted on his map.

Before their departure, Bering had prepared an elaborate code of signals, with flags and cannon and swinging lanterns at night, so that the sister ships could communicate with each other. On the second day out, three guns were fired by the *St. Paul*, and the ordinary flag was flown from her top-foremast crosstrees: the sign that Captain Chirikov wished to speak to the *St. Peter*. Lieutenant Waxell, in acting command, fired one gun in acknowledgment, and the two packets drew together. Through a speaking trumpet, Chirikov announced curtly that the *St. Peter* was steering southward of the agreed course, and suggested that he had better lead the way. It was an insulting message, and meant to be, but Bering did not take offense when Waxell brought the word to his cabin. Instead, he requested Waxell to signal the *St. Paul* to take the lead, in hopes that his Russian subordinate would be mollified and make no further trouble.

Day after day the Captain Commander remained in his bunk, his vacant eyes fixed on the deckbeams overhead, and left the entire conning of the ship to Waxell. He felt no excitement as he embarked on this climactic adventure of his life; all his earlier enthusiasm had been eroded away by the decade of suspicion and petty bickering. Now at last his ships were launched, and there could be no more nagging orders from St. Petersburg; and he surrendered to a deep despondency. It was more than a mental collapse. Lately his legs had commenced to swell painfully from some mysterious malady which Steller could not diagnose.

Steller was his only source of comfort. He had come to look on his youthful cabinmate as his own son, and extended to him the shy affection of a big inarticulate man, groping clumsily for words to express himself. Sometimes, as he lay on his back in the narrow cot, an arm would fall sideways with the open palm upward, as though he were reaching for a friendly hand. Steller did not respond to the mute appeal. It was not ingratitude; he was too engrossed in his scientific interests, and he had a young man's impatience with the weakness of age. For all his many-sided talents, he lacked the quality of compassion.

He was all over the ship, criticizing the officers, offering gratuitous advice on navigation although he had never before been to sea. At first the crew regarded him with good-natured indifference, like a pack of big mastiffs when a small dog walks stiff-legged and bristling among them. He was a head shorter than the burly Russian sailors; perhaps his assertiveness was an effort to compensate for his inferior stature. His positive manner amused them, and they made fun of him, putting on a mock show of saluting him when he approached and calling him "The Little Commander." Steller, who was abnormally sensitive about his height, reacted to their jibes with stinging sarcasm; and their earlier amusement hardened into sullen dislike. Only the fact that he shared Bering's cabin, and had the inner ear of the Captain Commander, kept them from open hostility.

The favorable winds continued all that week, and on June 12, eight days after leaving Avacha Bay, they were at latitude 46°. Frequent soundings were taken as they approached the supposed location of Gama Land, but no bottom was found at 90 fathoms, and sailors "looked from the crosstrees for land between S and W, and also S and E, but saw no land." The ships came together, and Waxell and Chirikov held another consultation through the speaking trumpets. Since they had reached the 46th parallel, the southernmost point agreed on at the council, it was decided to abandon the search for Delisle's mythical continent, and steer E by N directly for America.

Steller had been peering over the rail at the calm ocean, and had observed "various kinds of seaweed suddenly drifting about our ship in large quantities, especially the sea oak, which do not as a rule occur very far from the coast, inasmuch as the tide always carries them back to the land." He also noticed a number of gulls and terns and harlequin ducks, which the Russians called *kamenushkas;* he had previously seen these ducks in the freshwater streams of Kamchatka, and assumed that their presence indicated the proximity of land. He was wrong for once; the nearest land to the south was New Zealand; but he insisted to the officers that "if the initial course (ESE) were continued still farther, land would be reached shortly." The officers ignored his advice, and Steller grew indignant. Had he not shown them irrefutable proof, the gulls, the *kamenushkas*, the sea oak? Khitrov shrugged and spat over the side. "The Russian navy does not navigate by seaweed." Furious at their obtuseness, he carried his appeal over their heads to Bering. The Captain Commander, too exhausted to argue, turned his face to the wall; and Steller resorted to his caustic pen.

"Just at the time when it was most necessary to apply reason in order to attain the wished-for object," he wrote in his journal, "the erratic behavior of the naval officers began. They commenced to ridicule sneeringly and to leave unheeded every opinion offered by anybody not a seaman, as if, with the rules of navigation, they had also acquired all other science and logic. And at a time when a single day — so many of which were afterwards spent in vain — might have been decisive for the whole enterprise, the course was suddenly changed to north."

Now the weather began to turn sour, with mist and intermittent rain. A heavy reefing wind compelled the ships to reduce their canvas. The wind built to gale proportions, and a thick fog blotted out the sea. Early on June 20, the *St. Paul* was forced to heave to, and the *St. Peter* passed her about ten miles distant without seeing her.

It had been agreed that if the two ships were separated, they would rendezvous at the spot where they had lost contact.

The *St. Peter* put about, and returned to a point between the 50th and 49th parallels. For several days Bering's vessel combed the area with lookouts doubled, firing its cannon vainly over the empty ocean. The sister ships never sighted each other again.

When Chirikov discovered that the *St. Peter* had disappeared, he made a brief effort to find her, but it was largely perfunctory. Chirikov had not forgotten the vacillation and extreme caution which Bering had displayed on the earlier voyage to East Cape, and had lost all confidence in the Captain Commander. By nature he was cold and contriving, highly intellectual but ruthless in furthering his own ambition. He resented his subordinate position on the expedition; he had felt from the start that he should be the leader. Here was his excuse to be rid of Bering and on his own, to win fame and reward as the discoverer of Bolshaya Zemlya. After all, this was a Russian enterprise, and it rankled to see a Dane get the credit. A council of his officers, including de la Croyere, supported his decision to abandon the search for the other packet, and the *St. Paul* set its course ENE half E toward America.

De la Croyere's only thought was to get the voyage over and done with as soon as possible. A poor sailor, he had been seasick ever since their departure from Petropavlovsk, and was pasty-faced and thoroughly miserable. He had no stomach for the ship's diet of jerked reindeer beef and salted fish, and even his perfumed handkerchief was unable to offset the odor of the bilge that permeated the vessel. He made no attempt to take astronomical readings; his pendulum clocks were out of order, and there was no one to repair them. He stayed below, drowning his sorrows in vodka and regretting the day he ever left the pampered life of St. Petersburg.

The wind had turned fair and the *St. Paul* was making

good speed, gradually shaping her course a little more to the north. By July 12, signs of land appeared: a shore duck, a gull, two floating trees. Chirikov did not shorten sails, but the lead was heaved at frequent intervals during the night. At three in the morning of July 15, in latitude 55° 21′ N and longitude from Vaua 61° 55′, a range of high wooded mountains loomed against the gray sky: the Alexander Archipelago of southeastern Alaska.

Daylight revealed the islands more clearly. Large flocks of murrelets and pelagic cormorants swept past the ship, and bald eagles rose from the shore and circled overhead. The small boat was lowered to take soundings and seek an anchorage, but it returned that afternoon to report that the coast at that point afforded no protection from south and west winds. The boatswain added that "he saw large fir, spruce, and pine trees on the beach, many sea lions on the rocks, but no sign of human beings or their habitations." That evening the wind rose, and the *St. Paul* stood northwestward under short sail along the shore of what is now Baranof Island. For several days the storm continued, and rain and fog obscured the land; but by July 18 the clouds lifted, and in latitude 57° 50′, they saw a break in the rocky coastline.

"At 3:30 in the afternoon we went as close to the shore as we dared," Chirikov's daily journal recorded. "We sent the yawl ashore in charge of Fleet Master Dementiev who had with him ten armed men. He took with him a hand compass, a small lead, two empty water casks, a grapnel and a cable. He was told to make for the opening which seemed to us a bay and to take its bearings." The yawl also carried provisions for a week, a small copper cannon, and two rockets, with instructions to signal with one rocket when the boat landed.

It was a forbidding coast, boulder-strewn and sinister. From where the *St. Paul* lay, the crew lining the rail could see the narrow entrance to the bay, a churning gut of giant tide rips and whirlpools. They watched the yawl disappear behind some wave-washed rocks, and Chirikov waited for the expected signal. No rocket was seen, no sound of cannon heard. Five anxious days went by without any word from the shore party. On July 23, smoke was observed on the beach. "The fire burned in the very place into which the boat went," his journal stated, "and we took it for granted it was kept up by our men, and we fired seven times at intervals as a signal for them to come out, but no boat appeared, although the weather was fair. We noticed, however, that after we signalled the fire on the beach grew bigger."

Chirikov concluded that the boat must have been damaged and could not return, and he sent his only other boat with a carpenter and a calker and the necessary tools to repair the yawl. Boatswain Savelev and a sailor volunteered to handle the small boat, and Savelev was likewise provided with rockets and instructed to "leave the carpenter and calker ashore and return without delay to the ship with Dementiev and as many others as he could accommodate." The small boat was seen to enter the tide rips at the mouth of the bay, but no signal came from shore, and it did not return.

The *St. Paul* worked its way toward land, so close that "we could see the rocks and the surf playing on them," but still there was no sign of the boats. "We fired a gun as a summons to the men ashore; at the time there was hardly any wind, the ship was making almost no headway, and those ashore had the weather in their favor for coming out." They observed another fire on the beach, as if in answer to their gun. Cannon were sounded every hour during the night, and lanterns were hung at the ensign staff and at the gaff to guide the missing party if they returned.

Early in the morning of July 25 two boats were seen approaching them from the bay, one large and the other small. "We naturally thought they were our boats, and we stood toward them. When the small boat drew close to us, we became aware that it was not our boat, for it had a sharp bow, and those in it did not row with oars but paddled. The boat did not, however, come near enough so that we could see the faces of those in it. One of them had on clothes of red material. Being that far away they stood up and shouted twice "Agai, agai," waved their hands, and turned back to shore. I commanded my men to wave white kerchiefs to invite those in the boat to come to our ship. . . . They continued to pull away and finally disappeared in the bay from which they had come. We then became convinced that some misfortune had happened to our men, for it was the eighth day since the Fleet Master had left. . . . The fact that the Americans did not dare to approach our ship leads us to believe that they have either killed or detained our men."

Their fate has remained a mystery for two centuries. Rumors of a lost colony of Russians living on Baranof Island still persist, and an ancient folktale among the Tlingit Indians relates that the leader of the tribe, Chief Anahootz, dressed himself in the skin of a bear and played along the beach, luring Chirikov's shore party into the woods where the savages slaughtered them to a man. They are legends, and nothing more. The assumption that the men were murdered seems hardly probable; the natives had never seen a white man before, and would have been more apt to run away than attack. Moreover, ten armed men would have made some show of defense, and the *St. Paul* was near enough for those on board to hear the discharge of a musket. The appearance of the two canoes, which Chirikov felt was an indication of their guilt, could as easily be interpreted as proof of their innocence; if there had been an encounter, the natives would scarcely have exposed themselves to the larger body of Russians on the *St. Paul*. Their call of "agai" is strikingly similar to the Tlingit word "agou," which is a form of greeting, and might have been intended as a cry of warning.

A more plausible explanation is suggested by the experience of the explorer Laperouse, who cruised the Alaskan waters in 1786. He observed the narrow mouth of what is probably Latuya Bay, but the tides were so strong that he entered it only with the greatest difficulty. When his three small boats attempted to chart the bay, two of them ventured too near the mouth and were sucked into the strong current and lost. It is reasonable to assume that the same accident occurred in the opening which Chirikov discovered, now called Lisianski Straits, and that the Russians were swamped in the tidal rip and drowned before reaching shore. Even today the midway tide in Lisianski Straits rushes like a millrace, and the outer entrance can be safely navigated only at slack or low ebb.

Gradually the full extent of the disaster dawned on Chirikov. Not only had he lost nearly a quarter of his crew, but there were no small boats to go ashore and fetch fresh water. Only forty-five full casks were left in the hold, and Kamchatka was some two thousand miles away. The remaining water supply was strictly rationed, and the *St. Paul* started back under full sail for Avacha Bay.

Their progress was slow, with constantly shifting winds. The crew caught rainwater from the sails for drinking, and an attempt was made to distill the sea water, which was mixed with their dwindling supply of fresh water to overcome its bitter taste. On September 9 they sighted Adak Island, partway down the Aleutian chain, and anchored in a small bight, two hundred fathoms from the sloping treeless shore. A sparkling freshwater stream was running down the hillside, tantalizingly close, but there was no way to reach it. Some natives appeared on the beach and shouted to them; they could not make out their words because of the pounding surf. After an hour, they saw seven canoes approaching the ship, manned by islanders with double paddles.

"Each boat was about fifteen feet long," Chirikov noted, "the bow very sharp, the stern somewhat rounded and blunt, and the whole covered with hair seal and sea lion skins . . . except one spot between the center and stern, where there was a round hole in which the boatman sat. He was dressed in a kind of shirt which covered his head and his arms and was made from the intestines of a whale or some other animal. . . . When they were within fifty fathoms of the ship, they began to shout, turning first to one side and then to the other as the Yakuts do in their incantations. . . . We concluded they were praying that no harm might come to them from us."

Chirikov had ordered most of the crew to remain concealed below, with their guns loaded in case of attack; and he and his lieutenants stood on deck and tried to persuade the natives to come nearer. "We pressed our hands to our hearts as a sign that we would receive them in a friendly manner. To convince them still more, I threw them a Chinese cup as a mark of friendship." One of the natives picked it up, examined it, and tossed it into the water. Gifts of damask, small bells, needles, Chinese tobacco, and pipes were likewise spurned; evidently the natives had no idea what they were. "They did not even know that needles would sink and made no effort to keep them out of the water, but merely watched them go down."

The officers noticed several natives who "raised one hand to the mouth and with the other hand made a quick motion as if cutting something. This gave us the idea that they wanted knives, because the Kamchadals and other peoples of this region when they eat meat cut it at the mouth. I ordered that a knife should be given them, and when they saw it they were overjoyed and with great eagerness begged for more." Chirikov had found a means of bargaining, and he held up an empty water cask to indicate his need. Three natives paddled to shore, and returned shortly with skin bladders filled with fresh water, which were traded for more knives.

Their visit was cut short when a sudden squall sprang up, dragging the *St. Paul* toward the rocks which lined the shore. They were forced to cut the cable, losing their anchor, and stand out to sea. Week after week they fought unfavorable winds as they worked their way west along the Aleutians, sighting the Semichi Islands and the high land of Attu. The meager supply of fresh water they had obtained from the natives at Adak was soon exhausted, and the lack of properly cooked food and constant exposure to mist and rain broke the health of the crew. Scurvy, the bane of eighteenth-century mariners, made its dread appearance among the men. Several died, including Chirikov's two lieutenants and his navigator. De la Croyere, his resistance weakened by seasickness and heavy drinking, was near death. Even the Captain was stricken, and maintained command with the greatest difficulty.

By September 27, there were only six small barrels of water left, and those sailors who could still walk were so weak and emaciated that they could barely handle the ship. The sails and rigging were rotting and giving way when they sighted in the distance the three volcanoes which marked Avacha Bay, and made their way into the harbor on October 10. De la Croyere, who had kept alive with vodka during the voyage, dressed himself to go ashore in his embroidered silk waistcoat and powdered wig, and celebrated their safe arrival with the remainder of the brandy. His final excess was

too much; he died as the ship dropped anchor at Petropavlovsk, and was buried in all his Paris finery on the hillside
north of the settlement, ironically doomed to remain forever in
the surroundings which he loathed. Captain Chirikov never
recovered from his illness, and lived only a few years after his
return.

Bering had been deeply disturbed by the loss of contact
with the *St. Paul* on June 20, for he felt that the two ships
should remain together as a source of mutual aid in these uncharted waters. After cruising for three days in the area where
Chirikov's vessel had last been seen, a council of officers met in
his cabin and decided to sail back from the 50th to the 46th
parallel, on the possibility of sighting either Gama Land or
the *St. Paul*. By June 24 they were below latitude 46°, and
hope was abandoned of finding their sister ship. Now they
were satisfied that Delisle's land was "an invention of the map-
makers," Steller wrote, "over which either our ship or Captain
Spanberg's must have sailed if it had any real existence."
Twenty days had been wasted in the futile search, and they
could count on only six more weeks of good weather before the
fall storms set in. At noon on June 25, the officers of the *St.
Peter* voted "to carry out the original plan to sail between
north and east" toward America.

There was added urgency. Like Chirikov, they discovered
that their water supply was getting low; as early as the end of
June the rations of the crew had to be reduced. Weeks went
by without sighting Bolshaya Zemlya, but a lookout was kept
aloft at all times, and at night the ship drifted or moved under
little canvas. Once Lieutenant Waxell, gazing straight ahead,
noticed "something black on the water," he wrote, "covered
with an incredible mass of sea-birds of all kinds." Assuming it
to be a point of rock, he took a sounding without reaching

bottom. They altered course and passed the black object cautiously, and discovered that it was a dead whale. "You never feel safe," he observed, "when you have to navigate in waters which are completely blank."

The nerves of both officers and men were on edge, they were growing increasingly restless and irritable, and Steller's incessant arguments did little to improve their tempers. On July 10, he observed quantities of floating seaweed and clumps of land grass, as well as hair seals and "the Kamchatkan sea beaver, or more correctly sea otter . . . which lives entirely on crustaceans and shellfish and is therefore compelled to keep close to the shore." He concluded that these were signs of land not far to the north, and urged Waxell and Khitrov to set a more northerly course, but his suggestion was treated with contempt. "Draw us a map like Delisle's," Khitrov suggested.

Even the mild Bering rebuked him for making a nuisance of himself, and Steller commented acidly in his journal that the commander considered it "ridiculous, beneath his dignity and annoying to receive such advice from me, a man not versed in nautical matters." He added that "the brazen and very vulgar snubs by the officers, who coarsely and sneeringly rejected all well-founded and timely admonishing and propositions, thinking they were still dealing with cossacks and poor exiles freighting provisions from Yakutsk to Okhotsk, who had simply to obey and keep still without talking back, had been the cause of closing the mouth of myself as well as of others long ago."

By July 14, half the remaining supply of drinking water had been consumed by the crew, and what was left, even if the allowance were reduced, would not last longer than the end of August or early September. They did not know whether the barrels in the lower hold were full or whether some of their contents had leaked out. At a council of the officers, it was agreed to steer a north-northeasterly course until the twentieth, and if by that time they had not made landfall the attempt to find America would be abandoned and they would return home.

On Wednesday, July 15 — the same day that Chirikov caught his first glimpse of the islands of southeastern Alaska — Steller paced the forward deck, his eyes sweeping the northern horizon. The day was overcast, but a shifting wind fluttered the low clouds, occasionally parting them like curtains. Steller halted abruptly; for a moment his keen vision detected the faint outline of a range of mountains dead ahead. His shout of "Land!" brought the crew running to the bow, and they strained their eyes in the direction he pointed. Some were convinced they could make out the distant coastline, but they may have been swayed by their own eagerness. The officers were more skeptical; they had long since ceased to heed Steller, and made light of his claim, though they took the precaution of lowering the lead and found no bottom at ninety fathoms. Khitrov omitted any mention of the discovery in the ship's log. "Because I was the first to announce it," Steller sulked, "and because forsooth it was not so distinct that a picture could be made of it, the announcement, as usual, was regarded as one of my peculiarities."

The following morning was foggy, and the horizon was obscured. It started drizzling at noon, but a break in the clouds overhead permitted an observation of the sun, which showed the *St. Peter* to be in latitude 58° 14′ N. As the crew stared ahead, tense and expectant, the fog lifted without warning and revealed the mainland of America, a majestic panorama of "high snow-covered mountains," Khitrov noted in the log, "and among them a high volcano, N by W" (now Mt. St. Elias). "A point of the sighted shore which we named St.

Aphinogena bore N by E" (the bluffs just west of Yakutat Bay) "and another point of the same shore in NW, about 12 miles from us, we called St. Mariny" (Cape Suckling today).

The jubilation aboard the *St. Peter* was unbounded, and men embraced each other and wept with joy, or boasted of the bounty they would receive as the result of their discovery. "Now that we were close to land," Steller wrote, "it was great fun to listen to the conflicting expressions of self-conceit and expectations of future reward and pathetic effusions." Their exultant shouts roused Bering in his cabin, and he limped painfully on deck. His sagging gray face was expressionless as he gazed at the land for which he had sacrificed the prime years of his life. "Nobody failed to congratulate the Captain Commander, whom the glory for the discovery mostly concerned," Steller wrote. "He, however, received it all not only very indifferently and without particular pleasure, but in the presence of all he even shrugged his shoulders while looking at the land." Bering's great moment had come too late.

He turned and hobbled to his quarters again, and Steller and the draftsman Plenisner followed him, puzzled at the Captain Commander's strange apathy. Bering lay inert on his bunk, and his low halting voice carried an ominous note of prophecy.

"In the cabin," Steller entered in his journal, "he expressed himself to me and Mr. Plenisner as follows: 'We think now we have accomplished everything, and many go about greatly inflated, but they do not consider where we have reached land, how far we are from home, and what may yet happen. Who knows but that perhaps trade [westerly] winds may arise which will prevent us from returning. We do not know this country; nor are we provided with supplies for wintering.' "

He closed his eyes, and Steller, exasperated by the old man's forebodings, hurried back on deck.

IV. TEN YEARS FOR TEN HOURS

THAT AFTERNOON the wind dropped off to a dead calm, and they lowered the staysails and drifted with the strong easterly swells. The shoreline grew clearer with each slow creaking mile, and Steller could see the numerous bays and inlets, the scattered islands, the outer barricades of sharp pinnacle rocks. A gathering bank of low clouds obscured the coast by evening, but the peak of the volcano, higher than any he had observed in Siberia or Kamchatka, caught the last rays of the sun, and the perpetual snow on its summit changed gradually from fire red to salmon to a deep violet.

He was too excited to sleep, and he stood on the forward deck as the last light faded, staring ahead into the black unknown. What never-before-seen plants and birds and animals awaited him in this magic continent? What aborigines lurked in its primeval forests, what untold wealth in gold and minerals to be reported to an astonished world? His discoveries would dwarf all previous scientific achievements, and bring luster to the Academy's name and his own. He would return to St. Petersburg in triumph with a collection of natural wonders which would justify the ten long years of toil and expense. Surely, now that they had found America, Bering would not try to return to Avacha Bay this fall. The Captain Commander would see it as his duty, Steller was confident, to winter here in spite of hardships, and allow him time to explore all the secrets of Bolshaya Zemlya. He was still leaning over the rail at midnight when a breeze sprang up out of the north and the first raindrops pelted his cheeks.

It was stormy the following morning, with occasional heavy squalls that blotted out all visibility, and the *St. Peter* proceeded cautiously, swinging the lead every hour without finding bottom. All that day and the next they had to tack against contrary winds, and Steller groaned aloud with impatience. On Saturday afternoon they were close enough to the mainland for him "to view with the greatest pleasure the beautiful forests close down to the sea, as well as the great level ground in from the shore at the foot of the mountains. The beach itself was flat and, as far as we could observe, sandy." They kept the land to their right, and sailed in a northwesterly course to get under the lee of a high spruce-covered island, now Kayak Island, which they sighted on Sunday. Soundings showed fifty-five fathoms, and a bottom of soft bluish clay.

Steller had noticed a channel between the island and the mainland, and correctly deduced the presence of a "notably large stream," the present Bering River. Its current could be detected several miles off shore, and "the difference in the water could be inferred from the floating matter and the lesser salinity." He argued with the officers that it would be better to anchor in the channel, or perhaps in the protected mouth of the river itself. They spurned his advice, and Khitrov inquired with heavy sarcasm: "Have you been here before, that you are so certain?" At six o'clock on Monday morning, the *St. Peter* dropped its small bower anchor about a half mile off the island, to which Bering gave the name of St. Elias in honor of the saint of the day.

The Captain Commander had roused himself from his lethargy to come on deck, but he did no more than glance toward the land. His sole concern was the safety of his ship. First he must locate a sheltered harbor, then obtain fresh drinking water; after that there would be time to think of other things. He ordered Fleet Master Khitrov to take the longboat, with a crew and ammunition, and explore the straits in search of a more secure anchorage in case of a severe blow. The yawl would carry the watering party ashore to fill the casks.

Steller had been beside himself with eagerness for the past hour, waiting at the rail with his long-handled Yakut *palma* knife for digging up plants; but as he prepared to follow Khitrov into the longboat, Bering beckoned to him. "No, Mr. Steller. I cannot permit you to leave."

He did not understand. "I would not be in his way, sir. All I wish is to be dropped off on the mainland."

"Master Khitrov is not to waste time. He has his orders, and nothing must hamper him."

"But I have my orders also." Steller's voice grew shrill, a sign of mounting temper. "This is in the line of my principal work, my calling, my duty."

"You would be risking your life alone. No one knows whether there are hostile natives —"

"I have never been so womanish as to fear danger," Steller retorted, trying to control himself. "It is my determination to serve the Crown to the best of my ability." He saw the longboat pull away, its oars glinting in the sun. "I demand to be put ashore at once."

The sailors on deck had paused in their work, listening in shocked silence. If one of them had spoken thus to the Commander, he would have been clapped in irons. Bering was aware of the intent group gathered around them. "We'll discuss it later in the cabin," he suggested in a low voice, and rested a paternal hand on Steller's shoulder. The conciliatory gesture triggered a sudden explosion of rage. "I put all respect aside," Steller admitted in his journal, "and prayed a particular prayer." In the choicest epithets of his blistering vocabulary, he denounced Bering before the crew as a weakling and an old woman. "If for reprehensible reasons I am not given the permission," he threatened, "I will report this action to the Senate and Admiralty in the terms it deserves."

Bering gazed at him for a long moment, and then smiled. It was the bewildered, almost sheepish smile of a father whose favorite son has slapped his face in public. His manner was apologetic, as though he were trying to protect Steller by humbling himself. "You may go to the island with the watering party," he said quietly.

By ten o'clock the empty casks were loaded in the yawl, and Steller and his hunter Lepekhin climbed aboard. As they pulled away, Bering could not resist a sly impulse. He signaled to the two ship's trumpeters, Toroptsov and Vasiliev, and they stood by the rail and blew a loud flourish customary for a departing naval dignitary. Steller, who had no sense of humor about himself, was at a loss to "distinguish between mockery and earnest. . . . Without returning thanks, I accepted the affair in the spirit in which it was ordered," he wrote enigmatically, "as I have never been a braggart, nor would I care for such attentions even if they were really intended to honor me." With the brassy laughter of the trumpets ringing in his ears, he knelt in the bow of the yawl and scanned the approaching shore.

Kayak Island lies a couple of miles from the mainland, a narrow sliver of land about fifteen miles in length, running northeast and southwest. Spruces line the shore in solid ranks, and above their tops the central spine of the island rises to twelve hundred feet, a treeless ridge velvety with moss. The boatswain steered for a depression in the rocky beach, where a fresh clear stream emptied into the ocean. As the keel grated on pebbles, Steller leapt into the shallow water and splashed ahead of the others onto the gravelly sand. It did not occur to him that he was making history, that his footprints were the first ever left by a white man on Alaskan soil. He beckoned to Lepekhin to follow him, and set off along the beach at a half-run.

Everywhere the sand was gouged with the marks of hair seals which had dragged themselves up onto the beach to bask, and dotted with the excrement of numerous sea otters; proof to Steller that they were not hunted by the natives for food. Black and red foxes trotted at his heels, remarkably unafraid, and ravens and magpies fed undisturbed on sand fleas in the kelp. About two-thirds of a mile from the watering place, his sharp eyes detected the first sign of humans. "Under a tree I found an old piece of a log hollowed out in the shape of a trough, in which, a couple of hours before, the savages, for lack of pots and vessels, had cooked their meat by means of red-hot stones, just as the Kamchadals did. The bones, some of them with bits of meat and showing signs of having been roasted at the fire, were scattered about where the eaters had been sitting." He guessed that they were reindeer bones, though he observed no such animal on the island. More probably they were the bones of mountain goats, which still occur in large numbers in the St. Elias range.

Around the live coals were pieces of dried fish, which in Kamchatka "serves the purpose of bread," also blue mussels similar to those found in Kamchatka and eaten raw. In several large shells, evidently used as dishes, he found "sweet grass completely prepared in Kamchadal fashion, on which water

seemed to have been poured in order to extract the sweetness."
There were other clues to the identity of the natives. "The
chopped-down trees . . . were miscut with many dull blows
in such a way that in all likelihood the cutting must be done
by these savages, as in Kamchatka, with stone or bone axes."
More revealing, he discovered near the fireplace a wooden ap-
paratus "with which, for lack of steel, they make fire by fric-
tion." He felt sure "that this invention came from Kamchatka,
consequently that both peoples had intercourse with each
other or even that this people is one with the Kamchatkan and
has emigrated." His conclusion was strikingly accurate; the
natives around St. Elias were Eskimos of the Ugalakmuit
tribe, of Asiatic origin.

Steller and his cossack servant pushed on along the beach,
keeping a wary eye for ambush, and paused at a well-worn
path which led into the forest. Lepekhin had a loaded gun,
besides his hunting knife and axe but Steller was unarmed
save for his long-handled *palma*. He cautioned the cossack, in
case they encountered any natives, to do nothing without his
orders, and they started up the path in single file, Steller in the
lead. It was dark and dank under the giant spruces, and their
boots made no sound in the thick moss which covered the
ground and padded the roots and trunks of the trees, swelling
them to twice their normal size. Apparently the natives had
tried to cover up the trail as they fled, but their hasty efforts
only made it more conspicuous. Here and there he saw trees
stripped of their bark, and concluded it was used for houses or
storage sheds. After a short distance, the trail broke up into a
number of minor paths, and he explored them one by one until
he discovered a small clearing, spread with fresh-cut grass.

While Lepekhin stood guard with his musket primed, Steller pushed the grass aside, revealing a layer of rocks. Beneath
the rocks was a rectangle of tree bark laid on horizontal poles,

which covered a cellar hole twelve feet deep, filled with foods and artifacts. He lowered himself into the cellar and examined the contents swiftly; at any moment the natives might return and discover the intruders. Invisible eyes seemed to watch him from the surrounding forest as he listed the items in his pocket notebook: "(1) *Lukoshkas*, or utensils made of bark, filled with smoked fish of a species of Kamchatkan salmon called *nerka* (red salmon), so cleanly and well prepared that I have never seen it as good in Kamchatka, and it is also much superior in taste; (2) a quantity of sweet grass from which liquor is distilled; (3) different kinds of plants, whose outer skin had been removed like hemp . . . for making fish nets; (4) the dried inner bark from the larch or spruce tree done up in rolls and dried; the same is used as food in time of famine, not only in Kamchatka but all through Siberia and even in Russia; (5) large bales of thongs made of seaweed which we found to be of uncommon strength and firmness. Under these I also found some arrows in size greatly exceeding those in Kamchatka and approaching the arrows of the Tunguses and Tatars, scraped very smooth and painted black, so that one might well conjecture that the natives possessed iron instruments and knives."

He completed his inventory and, as proof of his discovery, took from the cellar two bundles of fish, some arrows, and a wooden implement for making fire. These he sent back by Lepekhin to the watering place, with instructions to forward them to the Captain Commander and request two or three men to help him in his search. "I also had those on shore warned not to feel too secure but to be well on their guard. I then covered over the cellar as it had been and proceeded, now all alone, with my project of investigating the most noteworthy features of the three kingdoms of nature until my cossack should return."

He had gone only a short distance when he found his way

blocked by a steep ledge, now known as Steller's Hill, which extended so far into the ocean that he could not follow the beach around its base. After much difficulty, he climbed to the summit, and discovered that its opposite side was a vertical wall, impossible to descend. There were no paths through the dense tangle of fallen spruces, and he realized that, if he went further inland, his cossack could not find him, and he would be too far from the others in case of trouble — "dangers which I should not have feared had I the least assistance of companions. . . . I turned my eyes toward the mainland to take a good look at least at that country on which I was not vouchsafed to employ my endeavors more fruitfully." He started back to the watering place "with real regret over the action of those who had in their hands the direction of such important matters."

As he worked his way down the side of the ledge, his heart skipped a beat. Less than a mile away, he saw a thin column of smoke rising "from a charming hill covered with spruce forest, so that I could now entertain the certain hope of meeting with people and learning from them the data I needed for a complete report." Overjoyed at this rare opportunity, he hurried to the beach, and found that the watering party had filled their casks and were about to row out to the ship. He sent an urgent message to Bering, reporting his find and asking again for "the small yawl and a few men for a couple of hours. Dead tired, I made in the meantime descriptions on the beach of the rarer plants which I was afraid might wither, and was delighted to be able to test out the excellent water for tea."

Perhaps no other naturalist in history ever accomplished so monumental a task under such difficulties and in so little time. It was four in the afternoon when Steller spread his specimens around him on the sand, and began to enter in his notebook the results of the previous six hours. When the yawl returned at five o'clock, he had completed his exhaustive report, the first scientific paper ever written on Alaskan natural history. The original manuscript still exists in the archives of the Russian Academy of Science, and a reproduction of the classic document is preserved in the United States Library of Congress.

Some plants in his collection were already familiar to him from his earlier investigations in Kamchatka. He identified the upland cranberry, the red and black whortleberry, and a shrub which he called the scurvy berry, probably the black crowberry. He was more enthusiastic over "a new and elsewhere unknown species of raspberry," the salmonberry of Alaska and the Pacific Northwest. Although the berries were not yet fully ripe, Steller was impressed by their "great size, shape, and delicious taste." He wrote bitterly to the Academy later: "This fruit . . . had well deserved that a few bushes of it should have been taken along in a box with soil and sent to St. Petersburg to be further propagated. It is not my fault that space for such was begrudged, since as a protestor I myself took up too much space already."

The yawl brought what Steller ironically described as "the patriotic and courteous reply" to his message to Bering, a brusque order to "betake myself on board quickly or they would leave me ashore without waiting for me." There were only three more hours till sunset, barely time to "scrape together as much as possible before fleeing the country." He sent Lepekhin to shoot some of the strange and unknown birds he had noticed, easily distinguished from the European and Siberian species by their particularly bright coloring, and he started down the beach in the opposite direction, returning at sundown with his botanical collection.

Lepekhin had equally good luck. He "placed in my hands a single specimen, of which I remember to have seen a likeness painted in lively colors and described in the newest account of the birds of the Carolinas." Steller's fantastic memory had recalled a hand-colored plate of the eastern American bluejay in Mark Catesby's *Natural History of Carolina, Florida, etc.*, which he had seen years before in the library of the St. Petersburg Academy; and he identified Lepekhin's find as its west coast cousin, known today as *Cyanocitta stelleri*, or Steller's Jay. Now his last doubts about the land they had discovered were resolved. "This bird proved to me that we were really in America."

On his return to the watering place, he was met with a final command that, unless he came on board at once, no more notice would be taken of him. He stowed his precious specimens in the yawl and hastened back to the *St. Peter*, prepared for a stern rebuke from the Captain Commander. Instead, to his great astonishment, he was greeted affably and offered a cup of hot chocolate, an exotic luxury which had been brought all the way from St. Petersburg in order to celebrate the discovery of Bolshaya Zemlya. Mollified, he suggested to Bering that some gifts should be left at the cellar hole in exchange for the items he had taken, and the boatswain was instructed to carry ashore an iron kettle, strings of beads, silk, a pound of leaf tobacco called *shar*, and an iron Chinese pipe. Steller pointed out that tobacco was unknown to the natives, and "it might occur to them to eat it." He urged that knives or hatchets would be more welcome, but "to this it was objected that such presents might be regarded as a sign of hostility, as if the intention were to declare war. How much more likely was it, particularly if they attempted to use the tobacco in the wrong way, for them to conclude we had intended to poison them."

Half a century later Commander Billings touched at Kayak Island, and an old native "remembered that when he was a boy, a ship had been close to the bay and had sent a boat ashore; but on its approaching the natives all ran away. When the ship sailed, they returned to their huts and found in their subterranean store room some glass beads, leaves, an iron kettle, and something else." He did not specify whether they ate the tobacco.

Khitrov and the longboat returned to the *St. Peter* an hour after Steller. Although he had seen no human beings, he reported, he had come across a small dwelling built of wood, the walls of which were decorated with small carvings and so smooth that it seemed to him they had been planed and prepared with cutting tools. From this building he brought a food receptacle of peeled bark, a whetstone with streaks of copper, a hollow ball of hard-baked clay which contained a pebble and was probably used as a child's rattle, a paddle, and the tail of a silver-tipped fox. His discoveries had been made on what is now Wingham Island; he had not dared set foot on the mainland for fear of the natives. In addition, he told the Captain Commander, he had located a landlocked harbor where the ship might lie in perfect safety.

Bering received his information without comment, and limped back to his cabin, weighing the momentous decision that faced him. Now he must make up his mind whether to linger in these strange waters, or set sail for home. It was hard to concentrate on the problem. His mood of depression, which he had thrown off during the day, settled on him again; he was confused and irresolute, and his attention kept wandering. The swelling of his feet had been increasing lately, and the pain distracted him. He packed his clay pipe with coarse Chinese tobacco and sat on the edge of his bunk, trying to marshal his thoughts.

Steller was working at a small table opposite, sorting and cataloguing his specimens by the light of a swinging whale-oil lamp. He seldom used tobacco, and the rank smoke from his cabinmate's pipe gagged him. He glanced up irritably, and found the older man's eyes on him, somber and troubled. They had barely spoken since he returned to the ship; he had not forgiven Bering for his peremptory recall. The Captain Commander seemed to read his mind.

"I know your desire to remain a little longer, Mr. Steller." For all their intimacy, they had never been on a first name basis; Bering's Danish reserve and Steller's German-born sense of discipline had erected a formal barrier between them. "You would like to continue your research ashore, but there are other matters to consider. Remember it was decided at the council in Petropavlovsk that we should return to Avacha Bay by the middle of September. The *St. Peter* has been seven weeks coming this far; it is safe to assume that our homeward trip will take as long, God knows maybe longer. With the approach of the monsoon season, the prevailing winds may shift to the southwest contrary to our course, and autumn storms might delay us further. Even under the most favorable conditions, we would have only three spare weeks to carry out the instructions of the Admiralty and chart the American coast before sailing back to Kamchatka."

"But we have not yet seen the natives, sir. We could bring back information about a primitive race on whom no European has ever looked. Give me a few more days to explore."

Bering took a long drag on his pipe before he replied. "Your official position is listed as mineralogist," he said frankly, "and what was the result of your exploration today? Some birds, a few trinkets from a native cellar, an accumulation of plants which take up valuable space on our crowded ship. The birds and plants will still be here when the country is visited again. This year we should be satisfied with the discovery already made." He was thinking aloud, trying to convince himself as well as Steller. "To be sure, we have not yet filled all our water casks, but there should be enough for our return voyage."

"Then our only purpose is to bring American water back to Asia?"

"As commander of this expedition, Mr. Steller, I am responsible for its safety." Bering had a seaman's sixth sense about weather. "The wind is favorable now, but it may turn against us tomorrow."

Steller saw that it was useless to argue. His own conception of the meaning of their voyage was diametrically opposed to that of the Captain Commander. To Bering, scientific data was of minor importance; their main objective was to locate America on the map, to survey its position for future navigation, to establish the Russian Empire's claim to this newfound land in the Pacific. They would never be able to understand each other's point of view, Steller realized. "It was quite plain that we had nothing in common," he wrote, "and nothing to keep us united except that we were locked up together on the same ship."

He stretched out on his berth, exhausted after his strenuous day ashore, and was instantly asleep; but Bering lay wide awake in his bunk, smoking and pondering the problem. Sometime in the small hours of the night he reached his decision. Shortly before daybreak on Tuesday the Captain Commander appeared on deck and, without calling a ship's council, ordered the surprised crew to weigh anchor at once. Both Waxell and Khitrov pleaded with him to delay until the remaining twenty water casks could be filled, but Bering, having once made up his mind, refused to listen. Perhaps he knew that, if he faltered, his brief moment of resolve would be over. Main topsail and foresail were set, and the *St. Peter* stood out of the bay, gradually gaining the sea.

Steller watched the enchanted coastline fall away behind them. All his life he had waited for this opportunity, and now it was lost forever. He made a despondent entry in his journal: "The only reason why we did not attempt to land on the mainland is a sluggish obstinacy, a dull fear of being attacked by a handful of unarmed and still more timid savages, and a cowardly homesickness. . . . The time here spent in investigation bears an arithmetical ratio to the time used in fitting out; ten years the preparation for this great undertaking lasted, and ten hours were devoted to the work itself."

V. A SOUND OF GUNFIRE

BERING's premonition proved all too accurate. Wednesday was "stormy, squally, rainy," with a strong wind. Clouds concealed the coast, the sky sat solidly on the sea, and for several days they were off soundings. On the morning of July 25, Khitrov's log recorded, the Captain Commander "had a consultation with his officers, and it was agreed while the gloomy weather lasted to hold the course SW in order to keep off the land, about which we know nothing, but in clear weather to hold a W by N course in order to see the mainland."

For a week they groped their way blindfold with no charts to guide them, no sun or stars to establish a navigational fix. Sometimes they guessed they were close to shore; they would sail for two or three hours through a stretch of calm water, evidently under the lee of an invisible island to the north, then suddenly they would pass its western point and encounter waves so powerful that they could scarcely manage the vessel.

The more they sought to avoid the land, the more it seemed to pursue them, looming perversely out of the fog in their direct path. "On the occasions when we had a good wind and, all unsuspecting, adjusted our course," Lieutenant Waxell recalled, "we sighted land on either quarter and so had to put out to sea again, thus having to treat a favorable wind as though it had been a headwind."

Waxell had seldom left the wheel since the helpless Captain Commander had turned over to him the full responsibility for the *St. Peter*. He was a lanky lantern-jawed Swede, who might have been called handsome except that his features were overlarge and the eyes set a little too close together. A soft tawny beard covered his chin, partly concealing the deep clefts that creased his face on either side of the mouth when he smiled. He was stubbornly honest, and frank to admit his youth and lack of experience in commanding a ship; though in fact he was by far the most capable seaman aboard, and drove himself doggedly to set an example for the disheartened crew.

The silence and solitude was beginning to oppress them. Their eighty-foot packet was a dot in space, the only ship in an immense and fogbound ocean. They passed the entire length of Kodiak without seeing it, but toward evening on August 1 the mist thinned a little. The moon was in its last quarter, and a little after midnight, in the dim light, a lookout in the crosstrees made out the black silhouette of an island dead ahead. They had almost run aground in the dark. "It was discovered on sounding that the ship was in four fathoms of water," Steller wrote, "though it was reported differently to the Captain Commander." All hands worked desperately to bring the *St. Peter* about, but the sailors were strangely listless, stumbling into one another and barely able to haul the lines. Despite their peril, some could not even rouse themselves to come on deck.

"We tried everything possible to escape from there," Waxell stated, "but in whatever direction we sailed, we found only shallow water. I had no idea what was the best thing to do; nor would it have been advisable to have dropped anchor without knowing the distance from land; especially not as there was a strong wind and the seas were running high." He gambled on sailing due south; for an agonizingly long time the soundings remained the same, but at last they came into deeper water, furled the sails, and dropped the bower in eighteen fathoms.

Dawn showed them to be only two miles from a large wooded island, which Waxell named Foggy Island, but which the later explorer Vancouver renamed Chirikov Island, despite the fact that Chirikov never sighted it. Toward noon a sea lion appeared near the ship, and Steller watched it "swim continuously around it for more than half an hour. I asked the Captain Commander, as the wind and weather were favorable, to let me go ashore for a couple of hours in the small boat to continue my investigations, but we got into a slight altercation on the subject, with the result that he finally called a sea council in which it was agreed that in the future nobody should upbraid me, as if I, on my part, had not wanted to do my duty most zealously . . . this everybody promised, and I let it go at that." Steller was determined not to leave empty-handed, however, and before their departure he lowered a hook over the side and caught two unknown species of sculpins. "I made at once a description of them and preserved them in spirits, but they, along with other rare collections, were lost during the disastrous stranding of the vessel in November."

On August 3 they made out the snow-clad peak of Mt. Chiginagak, which marks the beginning of the Alaska Peninsula; next day they were among the Semidi Islands; the ship seemed to be "hemmed in by land all around," and the officers decided to sail still farther south. They were making little or no progress; the favorable easterly winds had shifted to westerly, as Bering feared, and they were forced to tack constantly, or heave to in order to ride out a severe squall. "During this time," Steller noted, "we saw large numbers of hair seals, sea otters, fur seals, sea lions, and *Sturmfische* [porpoises]. . . . Whenever these animals were to be seen unusually often in a very quiet sea, a storm followed soon after; the oftener they came up and the more active they were, the more furious was the subsequent gale."

South of the Semidis, shortly before sunset on August 10, Steller's eye was attracted by "a very unusual and unknown sea animal" — the mysterious "sea monkey" whose identification has been a source of endless argument for two centuries. "It was about two Russian ells [five feet] in length," he wrote, "the head was like a dog's, with pointed, erect ears. From the upper and lower lips on both sides whiskers hung down, which made it look almost like a Chinaman. The eyes were large; the body was longish, round and thick, tapering gradually toward the tail. The skin seemed thickly covered with hair, of a grey color on the back, but reddish white on the belly; in the water, however, the whole animal appeared red, like a cow. The tail was divided into two fins, of which the upper, as in the case of sharks, was twice as large as the lower. Nothing struck me as more surprising than the fact that neither forefeet (as in the marine amphibians) nor, in their stead, fins were to be seen."

He was particularly impressed by "its wonderful actions, jumps, and gracefulness. For over two hours it swam around our ship, looking, as with admiration, first at the one and then at the other of us. At times it came so near to the ship that it could have been touched with a pole, but as soon as anybody stirred it moved a little farther. It could raise itself one-third of its length out of the water exactly like a man, and sometimes it remained in this position for several minutes. After it had observed us for about half an hour, it shot like an arrow under our vessel and came up again on the other side . . . in this way it dived perhaps thirty times. There drifted by a seaweed, club-shaped and hollow at one end like a bottle, toward which, as soon as it was sighted, the animal darted, seized it in its mouth, and swam with it toward the ship, making such motions and monkey tricks that nothing more laughable can be imagined. After many funny jumps and motions it finally darted off and did not appear again. It was seen later, however, several times in different places of the sea."

This fantastic creature has never been observed since, and naturalists have offered various theories to explain the phenomenon. Some claim that it was the product of Steller's vivid imagination, others that he saw a sea otter or bachelor fur seal and in the uncertain light mistook it for a new species. This would seem highly unlikely; he studied the animal for two hours, sometimes at close enough range to have "touched it with a pole." As trained and exact a scientist as Steller could scarcely have confused it with an otter or seal, particularly since his journal mentions that he had seen both of them previously; nor was he given to erratic flights of fancy. The simplest explanation is that the "sea monkey" actually existed, and that Steller saw it for the first and last time before it became extinct, like the northern sea cow which he was the only naturalist ever to observe.

Early in August they learned the reason for the increasing lassitude and inefficiency of the crew. The assistant surgeon, Betge, reported an outbreak of scurvy aboard the *St. Peter*; five men were totally unfit for duty, and of the others sixteen were badly affected. This insidious scourge of sailing men is aggravated by lack of fresh food and constant exposure to dampness and cold. The victim suffers from extreme weariness, coupled with a feeling of depression, and he loses weight and becomes anemic and listless. The gums swell and grow spongy and bleed; the breath is fetid; there are hemorrhages into the muscles and joints, the spleen enlarges, and ulcers develop. Presently he can no longer move about and lapses into a dull stupor, content to lie in his bed and befoul himself. In the final stages of the disease, it is hard to distinguish between the sick and the dead.

Bering's strength had already been sapped by his recurrent malady, and his weakened condition made him an easy prey to scurvy. He was confined to his bunk, unable to stir; and Waxell and Khitrov and first mate Hesselberg met in his cabin to discuss their present critical situation. Although they had previously decided to spend more time investigating the American coastline, they pointed out, the persistent headwinds and fog, together with the epidemic which had invalided a number of the crew, called for a drastic change in plans. The officers proposed to abandon their exploration, and steer direct for Avacha Bay "along the 53rd parallel of latitude, or as near to it as the winds will permit."

The Captain Commander nodded silent assent; it was too much effort for him to speak. Their decision was read to the petty officers "down to the boatswain's mate," and all agreed. Steller was not consulted "as usual," he complained; and he insisted in vain that they could avoid the headwinds by following a more southerly course. "If I may now draw the logical conclusion between the object of the sea council and their subsequent acts," he scoffed, "it must certainly be as follows: 'These gentlemen want to go home, and that by the shortest road but in the longest way.'"

Home seemed impossibly far away. Three weeks had elapsed since they left Kayak Island, whereas with prosperous winds the distance could have been sailed in a tenth the time. Now September was almost on them, and they were still over twelve hundred miles from Kamchatka. Days were wasted zigzagging back and forth against the adverse gales, or drifting helpless in the teeth of a violent equinoctial storm. Sometimes they were blown far back to the east, and lost all the ground they had gained. They thought of themselves as forgotten ghosts, doomed to haunt these lonely seas forever.

Only twenty-six casks of fresh water remained in the hold; and at their average rate of progress of seventeen nautical miles a day, they estimated, it would take them two and a half months to reach Avacha Bay. Another ship's council was held on August 27, and it was decided to sail on a northeast course toward land in order to replenish their drinking supply. "This would not have been necessary," Steller was quick to remind them, "had we filled at St. Elias those twenty empty barrels which, without reason, were left behind." On the afternoon of the twenty-eighth, as they beat north, he detected increasing signs of land "such as sea lions, a species of cod which lives on the banks at a depth of 90 fathoms at the most, and a black gull," possibly a fulmar in its dark color phase. The following morning they sighted five bleak and treeless islands, and stood toward them, sending the yawl ahead to look for a safe anchorage with a good holding bottom. Late on August 29 — forty days after departing Kayak Island — the *St. Peter* dropped anchor in the narrow strait between Nagai and Near islands in the Shumagin group, off the Alaska Peninsula.

At daybreak Hesselberg was dispatched in the longboat to look for water, and Master Khitrov, his thick lips curled in an ingratiating smile, invited Steller to accompany the party. Steller was sure that this unexpected courtesy masked an ulterior purpose; during the night a bonfire had been observed on Turner Island, a couple of miles away, and he suspected that the Fleet Master was planning to visit the spot where the fire had been "in hopes that the naval officers might have the honor for the expected discovery" of the first American natives. He knew it would do no good to protest. "Although it was easy to perceive their intention, I nevertheless accepted their offer very kindly and went ashore with the water carriers," expressing the pious hope "that both parties might discover something useful, although there was little of that to be expected on a bare and wretched island."

No sooner had the longboat pulled away than Khitrov asked Waxell for permission to take the yawl and investigate the fire-builders. Waxell had good reason to distrust Khitrov's seamanship and was reluctant to let the small boat go so far away, since he doubted it could get back to the ship in the event of a sudden storm. The Fleet Master was obdurate, and demanded that his request be entered on record in the log book; and Waxell resolved to put the whole matter up to the Captain Commander. Bering, aroused from his stupor, replied weakly that "if Khitrov is anxious to undertake this investigation he may be allowed to do so, and to take with him such men of the crew as he himself may select." Khitrov embarked triumphantly for Turner Island with four men and a Kóryak interpreter, carrying beads and Chinese silk to be distributed as presents if he encountered any natives.

Steller had brought with him Thoma Lepekhin and the ship's draftsman, Frederic Plenisner, who had been assigned to him as artist. As soon as the longboat landed on Nagai Island, he set off in search of wholesome water. He located several clear springs and hurried back to the beach, to find that the sailors were filling their casks from the nearest stagnant pool. The level rose and fell with the sea, and he found its contents brackish and alkaline; but the men had seen their officers treat Steller with contempt, and they ignored his objections. He insisted on sending a sample of the water to Waxell, warning him that it was bound to increase in salinity in the casks and its use would aggravate the epidemic of scurvy.

"Although in this matter I ought to have been listened to in my capacity of physician, and although so much damage, even our final misfortune, resulted from it," he protested in his journal, "nevertheless my proposition was rejected from the old overbearing habit of contradicting. The answer was: 'Why, what is the matter with this water? The water is good, fill up with it.' Even though in the meantime I had found a still nearer watering place than the beloved salty puddle and proposed it in case the spring water should not please, it should and must not be so, in order that they might deny me all sense and all knowledge."

It was a fatal error in judgment, and Waxell himself confessed it subsequently, though he tried to excuse his decision on the grounds that the ship was lying in an exposed anchorage and he wanted to replenish the supply as rapidly as possible. "The water was good," he contended, "but although taken from a lake there was, nevertheless, some sea water in it, brought by the tide which sometimes inundated the island." His stubborn refusal to listen to Steller cost the lives of over a third of the crew, but all he admitted was that its use resulted "in sickness and the loss of several of our men, who died."

Seeing that his efforts to convince the watering detail were useless, Steller left them and reconnoitered the little island. It was nothing but a jumble of high jagged rocks, covered with grass and dwarf willows. Even the smallest shrubs were so bent and interwoven by the prevailing winds that "it was impossible to find in the entire region a straight stick two feet long." There were no trees; Nagai is beyond the western limit of timber in Alaska. Foxes barked at him like dogs, marmots whistled from the ledges, and on the clay bank of an inland lake he noticed the tracks of a large wolf. Every stream and pothole was full of red sculpins and Dolly Varden trout. Waterfowl were in great abundance: his notebook listed swans, violet-green and white-crested cormorants, auklets, snipe, sandpipers, various kinds of gulls, Greenland pigeons (probably the pigeon guillemot), and both horned and tufted puffins. "Of land birds, however, I observed only ravens, flycatchers [more likely the dwarf thrush, since flycatchers are unknown in that part of Alaska], snowbirds, and willow ptarmigan."

The plant life was much the same as Steller had observed on Kayak Island. Red whortleberries and black crowberries grew in profusion, but his happiest find was a number of "glorious antiscorbutic herbs," such as gentian and spoonwort and other cresslike plants. Steller had protested at the beginning of the voyage that the ship's medicine chest was miserably supplied with "surgical remedies enough for four to five hundred men in case of a battle, but had none of the medicines most needed on sea voyages and serviceable against scurvy."

On his return to the *St. Peter* that night, he requested Waxell to furnish several men to help him collect enough remedial herbs for the stricken crew, but "even this proposition was spurned. Later, however, there were regrets enough, and when we had scarcely four abled-bodied men left on the vessel, I was tearfully begged to help and assist, which then, though with empty hands, I did to the utmost of my strength and means." He could not resist a final thrust: "It must also have caused even the coarsest and most ungrateful persons to take notice when the Captain Commander, who from scurvy and confinement had entirely lost the use of his limbs, was restored by me to such an extent simply by partaking of the fresh spoonwort that within eight days he could get out of bed and on deck again."

Taking advantage of the fine weather, the scurvy victims had been brought ashore during the afternoon in hopes they would revive in the fresh air and sunshine. The sudden transfer from the foul atmosphere of the hold was too much for one of the sailors, Nikita Shumagin, who expired as he was carried up onto the beach. His shipmates dug a grave and erected a wooden cross; today the group of islands bears the name of the first white man to be buried on Alaskan soil.

The following day the wind freshened, and that evening the longboat was sent to Nagai with orders to bring the sick men and all others back to the ship immediately. Steller and his party were located on the far side of the island, four miles distant, and they ran as fast as possible to the landing place. A high surf was crashing on the beach, and the scurvy sufferers were being loaded into the boat with great difficulty, all of them drenched to the skin. Steller and his companions had to wade waist-deep through the breakers in order to clamber aboard.

Midnight saw a northeast gale raging, and Waxell feared the anchors would not hold; but Khitrov and his men had not returned in the yawl, and he could not abandon them. As a precaution, Waxell had the men tuck double-reefs in the furled topsails and foresail. The *St. Peter* continued to pitch violently at anchor. By noon next day there was four inches of water in the hold, and a dozen crewmen had been added to the sick list. On the morning of September 1 the gale swung to the southeast, exposing the ship to its full force. Despite Khitrov's prolonged absence, Waxell was forced to shift anchorage to a more protected position off Near Island. Steller noted in his journal with malicious satisfaction: "I now thanked God that through the cunning of the naval men I had been kept away from his company."

Khitrov had been having his customary run of bad luck. He had landed on Turner Island and located the site of the fire, but had seen no natives. On the afternoon of the thirtieth, when he realized a storm was approaching, he had tried to return to the ship; but the heavy seas prevented him, just as Waxell had foreseen, and he attempted to land in the pounding surf of Nagai Island. Only the fact that he hoisted a sail and steered straight at the breakers saved the yawl from overturning. It was badly damaged in beaching, and the men were soaked and half frozen. They built a bonfire to warm themselves, and also to signal the *St. Peter.* When they saw the ship getting under canvas, they concluded they had been left behind and were in despair. "He who could sleep, slept; and he who could not, wept till he was tired of weeping, and then he too fell asleep." It was not until September 2 that the sea was down sufficiently for Waxell to send the longboat ashore, and the stranded mariners were brought back to the ship, leaving their wrecked yawl on the beach "as a sort of offering on that American island."

For the past two days the wind had been holding southeasterly, but Waxell had been unable to take advantage of it because of Khitrov's absence. "If he had not gone at all," Steller wrote resentfully, "or if, on not meeting anybody he had returned betimes and thereby had not delayed the watering by depriving us of the yawl, we could have gotten out with the fair gale and been more than a hundred miles farther on our course. . . . Everyone grumbled because whatever that man touched, from Okhotsk on until the return voyage, had gone wrong and had brought misfortune."

The Fleet Master's bad luck was not yet over. "Master Khitrov, who had become uncommonly happy over his deliverance, took the lead in hand and at the first attempt left it on the bottom of the sea, which incident the common sailors interpreted as an evil omen and called to mind that just a year ago today the provisions were lost at the mouth of the Okhota through this same man's cleverness."

Sails were set and they steered for the open sea, but the breeze failed them and, realizing that they could not clear the point, they dropped the bower behind Bird Island. Another attempt was made to get around the island the following morning; again contrary winds forced them back, and the *St. Peter* hove to in the same spot as before, about four in the afternoon of September 4. "Through this event," Steller wrote, "it came about that without expectation or search we chanced to meet with Americans."

They had scarcely anchored off Bird Island when they heard a loud shout from the rocks, which at first they took to be the roar of a sea lion. A few moments later, two slender skin boats were seen paddling toward them from shore. Steller was struck by the resemblance of these canoes, which the Aleuts called *baidarkas*, to the kayaks of the Greenland Eskimos. "We all waited for them with the greatest eagerness and full of wonder. . . . When yet about half a verst distant from us both men in the boats began, while still paddling, simultaneously to make an uninterrupted, long speech in a loud voice of which none of our interpreters could understand a word. We construed it therefore as either a formula of prayer or incantation, or a ceremony of welcoming us as friends, since both customs are in use in Kamchatka and the Kuriles." This would seem to be the same native ritual observed by Chirikov at Adak Island.

As the *baidarkas* approached the ship, the crew lined the

rail, smiling and waving to indicate that the paddlers had nothing to fear. They paused, a short distance away, and gestured toward the land, pointing to their mouths and scooping up sea water with their hands as though inviting the white visitors to come ashore and have food and drink. Presently one of them drew a little nearer, and Steller saw that "before approaching quite close, he reached into his bosom, pulled out some iron- or lead-colored shiny earth, and with this he painted himself from the wings of the nose across the cheeks in the form of two pears, stuffed the nostrils full of grass," which caused them to bleed, "and then took from the sticks lying beside him on the skin boat one which was like a billiard cue, about three ells [seven feet] long, of spruce wood and painted red, placed two falcon wings on it and tied them fast with whalebone, showed it to us, and then with a laugh threw it toward our vessel into the water. I can not tell whether it was meant as a sacrifice or a sign of good friendship."

Lieutenant Waxell fastened two Chinese tobacco pipes and some glass beads to a piece of board and tossed it to the native in return. He picked up the gifts, looked them over carefully, and handed the board to his companion, who placed it on top of his *baidarka*. "After this he became somewhat more courageous, approached still nearer to us, though with the greatest caution, tied an eviscerated entire falcon to another stick and passed it up to our Koryak interpreter in order to receive from us a piece of Chinese silk and a mirror. It was not at all his intention that we should keep the bird but that we should place the piece of silk between the claws so that it would not become wet. However, as the interpreter held the stick fast and by it pulled the American together with his boat toward our vessel, the latter let go the stick, became frightened, and would not come so near again. Therefore the mirror and stick were thrown to him, with which they both paddled towards shore and beckoned us to follow."

The natives on the beach continued to shout and screech unintelligibly, and, after consultation with Bering, Waxell ordered the longboat lowered. He and Steller, together with the Koryak interpreter and nine sailors, rowed toward shore. In addition to bringing presents for the islanders, they took the precaution of providing themselves with lances, sabers, and muskets, which they covered with canvas in order to avoid arousing suspicion. To their disappointment the beach was rocky and, with the tide rising, Waxell was unwilling to risk smashing the ship's only remaining boat in the breakers. He dropped a grapnel some twenty fathoms away, and paid out the rope until the longboat was only fifteen feet from shore. "From the place on the beach where their boats and also our presents were lying scattered about unappreciated," Steller wrote, "both men and women, who because of the uniformity of the dress could hardly be distinguished from each other, all came to meet us at our approach, full of wonder and friendliness."

Since the longboat dared not go nearer the rocks, the interpreter and two sailors stripped off their clothes and swam ashore. The islanders seemed fascinated by the Russians' heavy black beards and hairy chests and limbs, "and led them by the arms, quite deferentially as if they were very great personages, to the place where they had been seated, presented them there with a piece of whale blubber, talked a bit with them, though nobody understood the other, and pointed at the same time frequently over the mountain, perhaps to indicate that they had come here on our account but that they had their dwellings on the other side," a guess which later proved to be correct when Steller sighted some sod huts as they sailed around the island. "A part of the islanders remained standing on the beach abreast of us, gazing at us without taking their eyes away and inviting us to them by beckoning."

Although Steller had little more than a quarter of an hour to observe the natives at close quarters, he missed no detail in his journal entry, the earliest known description of the Alaskan Aleuts. "They are of medium stature, strong and stocky, yet fairly well proportioned, and with very fleshy arms and legs. The hair of the head is glossy black, and hangs straight down all around the head. The face is brownish, a little flat and concave. The nose is also flattened, though not particularly broad or large. The eyes are as black as coals, the lips prominent and turned up. In addition, they have short necks, broad shoulders, and their body is plump though not big-bellied. All had on whale-gut shirts with sleeves, very neatly sewed together, which reach to the calf of the leg. Some had the shirts tied below the navel with a string, but others wore them loose. Two of them had on boots and trousers which seemed to be made after the fashion of the Kamchadals out of seal leather and dyed brownish-red with alder bark. Two had hanging on their belt, like the Russian peasants, a long iron knife in a sheath of very poor workmanship. . . . From the distance, I observed the nature of this knife very carefully as one of the Americans unsheathed it and cut a bladder in two with it. It was easy to see that it was of iron, and besides that it was not like any European product." Either the Americans had iron ore and knew how to smelt and work it, he reasoned, or they had traded the knives from the Chukchis.

He noticed further that "these people regard it as a special ornament to pierce holes anywhere in their faces, as we do in the lobes of the ears, and to insert in them various sticks and bones. One of these fellows had stuck a slate pencil, about 2½ inches long and exactly like those with which we write on ciphering slates, through the nasal septum. Another had a piece of bone stuck through crosswise above the chin just under the lower lip. Still another had a bone like it fastened in the forehead, and another, finally, had a similar one in each of the wings of the nose," just as the Chukchis wear "pieces of walrus teeth inserted in the nose and cheeks. . . . I observed also on all these Americans that they had a very scant beard, but most of them none at all, in which respect they again agree with the inhabitants of Kamchatka."

While they waited, an elderly native lifted his *baidarka* with one hand and carried it to the water, and paddled dexterously through the surf to the longboat. "He was made welcome with a cup of brandy, which, following our example, he emptied quickly, but also immediately spit it out again, and acted strangely, as if he did not seem to be any too well pleased with this fancied deception. Although I advised against such things as tobacco and pipes, our gentlemen opined nevertheless that the Americans had the stomachs of sailors and consequently, intending to neutralize the first displeasure with a new one, gave the stranger a lighted pipe of tobacco, which he accepted indeed, though paddling away quite disgusted. The smartest European would have done just the same if he had been treated to fly mushroom or rotten fish soup and willow bark, which the Kamchadals however consider delicacies."

The wind and surf were increasing, and Waxell ordered the three men back to the boat. The islanders let the two Russian sailors go, but were reluctant to yield up the Koryak interpreter, in whom they saw a resemblance to themselves in manner of speech and facial appearance. They offered him more whale blubber and iron-colored paint; when this failed to induce him to remain, they seized him and pinioned his arms behind him. He fought with all his strength, imploring Waxell to rescue him. At the same time, several overeager natives seized the painter of the longboat and tried to haul it ashore, evidently unaware that it would be dashed to pieces on the rocks.

Realizing that their situation was critical, Waxell ordered two muskets to be fired simultaneously into the air. As the thunder reverberated from the cliff, the terrified natives fell flat on the ground, dropping the painter and releasing the interpreter, who leapt into the water and swam to the boat. The sound of gunfire, heard in the Aleutians that day for the first time, would echo and re-echo through the islands for the next two centuries.

The grapnel had hooked itself fast under a ledge, and Waxell was obliged to cut the rope and leave it behind. As they rowed back to the ship, Steller observed that the islanders "at once rose up again, scolded us because we had rewarded their good intentions so badly, and waved their hands to us to be off quickly as they did not want us any longer." Some of them picked up rocks to speed their parting guests, but the longboat pulled out of range, and they had to content themselves with hooting and shrieking until the party boarded the ship.

The following morning, to everyone's surprise, nine natives in *baidarkas* paddled toward the *St. Peter* in single file, with the same shouts and incantations as before. "It must be assumed that powder and guns were unknown to them," Waxell surmised, "for they would hardly have come out to us again, and certainly not so close to the ship, if they had known that the two muskets I had ordered to be fired the previous evening were connected with things which could kill them." He added: "I could easily have taken all nine of the natives prisoner. I put such a plan to the Captain Commander, but I was given written instructions not to carry it out."

Two islanders approached near enough to grab hold of the side, and once more offered gifts of feathered sticks and face paint. "On their heads," Steller noted, "they had hats made of the bark of trees, colored green and red . . . the crown was uncovered, and they appeared to have been invented only for the purpose of shading the eyes from the sun. Between the hat and the forehead some had placed a few variegated falcon feathers, others tufts of grass, in the same manner as the Americans on the east side, about Brazil, decorate themselves with feather tufts. From these hats an argument might be derived for the supposition that the Americans came from Asia, because the Kamchadals and the Koryaks are in the habit of wearing exactly similar hats." The Russians exchanged a rusty iron kettle and five sewing needles for two of the hats. "On one of these there was fastened a small carved image, or sitting idol, of bone, with a feather sticking out from behind, intended no doubt to represent the tail."

The natives turned and paddled back to shore, apparently none too pleased with the results of their barter, and shortly afterward the *St. Peter* got under way, sailing around the eastern side of Bird Island past the sod village. The islanders had built a large fire and stood in a group on the beach, raising their voices in what Steller interpreted as a fond farewell. Waxell was more skeptical. "Whether this was to wish us a good voyage," he speculated, "or an expression of their joy at seeing us departing, on that I shall not express an opinion."

Everywhere the receding shore and the sea around them swarmed with waterfowl. Gulls and puffins and auklets circled the ship or rocked on the long green swells. Fulmars, which the Russians call *glupyshi* or stupid fellow, lit unconcernedly in the rigging. Steller took particular note of "an entirely black snipe with red bill and feet which constantly moved the head," the black oystercatcher of the Aleutians, and also a "very beautiful black-and-white pied diver never before seen," probably the ancient murrelet which, unlike other murrelets, stays in black and white winter plumage all year. Numerous whales played near the vessel, sometimes rising upright in the water for more than half their length, a sign that dirty weather was breeding.

They set their course southward to the 53rd parallel, in order to be clear of land. The wind was against them, westerly and WSW; autumn storms had begun, and turbulent seas compelled them to shorten sail. They had delayed too long. The eight days they had squandered in the Shumagins had sealed the fate of the *St. Peter*.

VI. "BY THE WILL OF GOD"

W EEK AFTER WEEK they battled headwinds that sometimes reached gale proportions, forcing them to reef
canvas. The constant lurching and tossing of the ship brought
added misery to the scurvy patients, and their moans could be
heard above the creaking of masts and steady snarl of wind in
the rigging. Many were in an advanced stage of the disease,
suffering from bloody fluxes of the bowels; but Steller had
been able to bring aboard only enough antiscorbutic herbs for
the Captain Commander, and was powerless to aid the rest.
The brackish water had already begun to turn saline in the
casks, as he had warned, and the roster of healthy men
dwindled rapidly.

In mid-September the log recorded another victim: "By the will of God died of scurvy the grenadier Andrei Tretyakov." A third of the crew was down by now, confined to the reeking hold, and the teeth of the other sailors were loosening. As the supply of fresh spoonwort gave out, Bering had a relapse and again lay helpless in his bunk, unable to move hands or feet. Even Waxell was showing the first signs of the plague, brought on by constant worry and the strain of sleepless nights. "I do not know whether there is anything more dreary or unpleasant in this world than thus having to navigate in an unknown sea," he recalled in his memoirs. "I can truthfully say that I did not get many hours' peaceful sleep during the five months. . . . I was in a continual state of uneasiness, always in danger and uncertainty."

Clouds hid the sun and the stars, and it was impossible to observe the latitude or correct their reckoning. On the afternoon of September 25, they were dismayed to see a pair of islands looming out of the fog, and a snowy volcanic peak in the distance: evidently Atka and Adak, where Chirikov had watered on his return trip, and the volcano on Great Sitkin Island. They did not know that the Aleutian chain curved southward, and had assumed they were far from any landfall. "It was most fortunate that we caught sight of the land while yet day," Steller wrote, "for otherwise we should certainly have run onto it in the night, or else, without any means of escape, have been driven by the wind and wrecked on it." They changed course hastily, and scudded south to a lower parallel.

Here the williwaw struck them two days later. All that morning the wind had been building in velocity, with a wild sobbing which culminated now and then in a high hysterical laugh. There was an insane quality in the sound that put their nerves on edge; it was the babbling singsong of a madman, without sense or reason. The fog had blown clear, and ragged wisps of cloud flicked overhead against a mottled brown and purple sky. The wind had been from the southeast, but suddenly at dusk it veered to the west, and they could hear a faraway rumble, the growl of a swollen river pressing against its dikes. They lowered the fore and main yards, and wallowed like a half-submerged log in the waves as the rumble grew louder. There was a hollow moment of silence, and then, as though a dam had burst in the sky, the full force of the williwaw thundered down on them.

"We could hear the wind rush as if out of a narrow passage, with such terrible whistling, raging, and blustering that we were in danger of losing masts or rudder or else of seeing the vessel broken by the waves, which pounded as when cannons are fired, so that we were expecting every moment that last stroke and death. Even the old and experienced pilot Hesselberg could not recall among his fifty years at sea having passed through a storm which even resembled it."

The tempest continued without letup all the next day, accompanied by lightning and hail. The *St. Peter* was being driven far back on her course, but they no longer cared about their position; their sole thought was to survive. On the twenty-ninth the wind swung to the southeast and seemed to abate, but toward ten o'clock at night it shifted once more to the west, and they could hear the same demented singsong and the approaching roar of another williwaw, more terrible than the first.

"On the 30th, about five in the morning," Steller recorded, "we encountered a storm of such redoubled violence as we have never experienced before or since; we could not imagine that it could be greater or that we should be able to stand it out. No one could lie down, sit up, or stand. Nobody was able to remain at his post; we were drifting under the might of God whither the angry heavens willed to send us. Half of our crew lay sick and weak, the other half were quite crazed and maddened from the terrifying motion of the sea and ship. There was much praying, to be sure, but the curses piled up during ten years in Siberia prevented any response. Beyond the ship we could see not a fathom out into the ocean because we continuously lay buried among the cruel waves. Under such conditions no one any longer possessed either courage or counsel."

At any instant they thought their tiny vessel would founder. Mountainous waves poised above her, toppled, and crashed on the frail deck with a stunning concussion. Her entire midsection was buried under tons of water, and men were flung headlong and carried along in the swirling foam, kicking their legs and grasping with upraised arm for a stanchion to keep from being washed overboard. The ship reeled from each successive blow as though she had been clubbed, staggering, falling forward, rising with a mighty effort, stumbling again. Sometimes the impact of a solid wall of water would halt her in her tracks, and she would quiver for a moment from bow to stern, give a deep convulsive shudder that racked her timbers till they groaned, and then plow solidly on her way.

The ruthless seas attacked her from all sides like a gang of street-fighters, kneeing her, stamping on her, clawing savagely at her superstructure. One of her deadeye lanyards tore loose; the fury of the wind ripped the ratlines; a bulwark was swept over the side. Below decks the hold was awash, and sick men were tumbled from their bunks and lay helpless in the foul-smelling water, sluicing from port to starboard with each roll of the ship. Some were face down, too feeble to right themselves, and their stronger companions hugged them and tried to hold their heads out of the muck. A dip of the bow slid the whole tangled mass of bodies forward over the slimy planks, and they brought up against a bulkhead with a thud and screams of pain.

Steller fought his way aft to the Captain Commander's cabin. It took all his strength to wrest the door open against the force of the gale. The interior of the cabin was a shambles: the shattered whaleoil lamp swung back and forth, sea boots and clothing were strewn in every direction, his chest had overturned and botanical specimens and papers mingled with spilled preserving fluid. Bering was lying half out of his cot, a limp arm draped on the floor. His open eyes were glazed, and for an instant Steller thought he was dead. He had to feel his pulse to be sure the heart was still beating.

He placed his lips close to Bering's ear, to be heard above the tumult, and shouted "Sir? Sir?" but the staring eyes did not move. Bracing himself against the pitch of the ship, he rolled the inert form back into the bunk, roped him securely in place, and stooped to gather up his scattered collection. A detonation like an explosion shook the vessel, and the cabin floor tilted at a forty-five-degree angle and he was slammed against the forward bulkhead as though by a heavy hand.

The helmsman had frozen at the wheel, and Waxell had seized the spinning spokes as the giant wave bore down on them. The white froth on its curling crest was so high above him that it seemed like snow on a mountain peak. He held the ship straight to meet it, and an avalanche of water blotted out the pilothouse. When he could see again, the *St. Peter* was hanging bow down on the rim of a cavernous trough behind the wave, ready to plunge headfirst into the sea. She teetered for a moment that was a lifetime, and then slowly, doggedly, her bow lifted again and she righted herself, green water streaming from her decks, and plunged ahead.

There seemed to be no end to the violence. One williwaw followed another, with rain and sleet and stinging hail. St. Elmo's fire played along the swaying crosstrees and rigging, and Steller observed in awe "the terrible rapid flight of the clouds which with incredible swiftness shot like arrows past our eyes and even met and crossed each other with equal rapidity." The crew was bruised and lame; some had deep cuts which had been cauterized by the salt water and did not bleed. They were numb with weariness, after a week of constant beating, and "the minds of all became as shaky as were their teeth from scurvy."

They had lost all track of the days. Khitrov's reckoning did not agree with the log, which was now being kept by second mate Yushin, and both were at variance with Steller's journal. On October 2, twenty-four petty officers and sailors were unfit for duty, and the others were experiencing stomach cramps from lack of food. It was impossible to cook in the heaving seas, and they subsisted on half-burnt biscuits, which were beginning to run short. "Deaths now became numerous," Waxell stated, "so much so that a day seldom passed without our having to throw the corpse of one of our men overboard." The entries in the log bore an ugly sameness: "By the will of God Alexei Kiselev died of scurvy." "Nikita Khanitonov died by the will of God." "By the will of God died the Yakutsk soldier Karp Pashennoi, and we lowered him into the sea."

On Sunday, October 25 — Khitrov says it was midafternoon, Steller early morning — a large island was sighted, "high, rocky, treeless, and covered with snow," probably the southern end of Kiska Island. Three days later, a few hours after the ship's cooper Buldirev expired of scurvy, another island rose out of the gray drizzle, "low and flat and with sandy beaches"; this is supposed to be the present Buldir Island, named for the dead man. Their drinking supply was down to a dozen casks, and Khitrov suggested that they drop anchor in the open sea and send the boat ashore for fresh water, ignoring the fact that not enough able-bodied crewmen were left to hoist the anchor again. His proposal was rejected, Steller observed in relief, for otherwise "we should assuredly altogether have found our graves in the waves." Even his expressive pen found it difficult to describe the misery aboard the *St. Peter.* "Not only did the sick die off, but those who according to their own assertion were well, on being relieved at their posts, dropped dead from exhaustion. . . . The cold, dampness, nakedness, vermin, fright, and terror were not the least important causes."

They had been blown all over the ocean, down below the 49th parallel, and back eastward nearly seven degrees of longitude. On the twenty-seventh, Yushin's log reported thirty-two men on the sick list, and he added: "I have such pains in my hands and feet, owing to the scurvy, that I can with difficulty stand my watch." The weather was growing bitter cold, with flurries of snow, and Waxell suggested to Bering that they might seek winter quarters in America. The Captain Commander was feverish and irrational. They must continue their homeward course, he insisted, and ordered that a collection should be taken among the Russians for the church at Petropavlovsk, and among the Lutherans for his family church in Denmark, as guarantee for a safe return.

Their situation grew more desperate as the month of October ended. "By now so many of our people were ill," Waxell stated, "that I had no one to steer the ship. Our sails, too, had worn so thin that I expected them to fly off at any moment. To bend on other sails was out of the question. I had not enough men for that. Indeed, when it came to a man's turn at the helm, he was dragged to it by two other of the invalids who were still able to walk a little, and set down at the wheel.

There he had to sit and steer as well as he could, and when he could sit no more, he had to be replaced by another in no better case than he. I myself was scarcely able to move about the deck without holding on to something. I could, perhaps, have set some sails myself, but what would have been the use, when there was none able to take them in again, should the situation make that necessary? . . . Those few who were still on their feet were dreadfully weak and exhausted, and so reluctant to do any work. Usually they begged to be released because they had but little strength left. Their only wish, indeed, was that a speedy death might free them from their miserable plight."

Terror had yielded to dull despair. None of them expected ever to see home again. They no longer thought of home as Russia — that was too far away and unreal to contemplate — but as the crude settlement at Petropavlovsk. On the thirtieth of October they sighted the Semichi Islands, at the western end of the Aleutian chain; but by this time they were so confused in their reckoning that they mistook them for the Kurile Islands which extend below Kamchatka to Japan. Instead of continuing due west, which would have brought them to Avacha Bay in another week, they set their course northward. Winter weather was setting in; spray froze as it fell, and each morning the decks and rigging were coated with ice. Five more of the crew died in as many days, only eight sailors were still able to move about, and Waxell was too wracked with scurvy to give orders. "Our ship was like a piece of dead wood, with none to direct it; we had to drift hither and thither at the whim of the wind and waves."

Shortly after eight o'clock on November fourth — Steller thought it was the fifth — a low range of jagged hills rose out of the ocean to the north, and the officers produced charts to prove it was the coastline of Avacha Bay. "It is impossible to describe how great and extraordinary was the joy of everybody at this sight," Steller wrote. "The half-dead crawled up to see it, and all thanked God heartily for this great mercy. The Captain Commander, who was a very sick man, became not a little aroused, and all talked of how, after having suffered such terrible misery, they were going to care for their health and take a rest. Little cups of brandy concealed here and there made their appearance in order to keep up the joy." Khitrov boasted loudly of his accurate navigation. "These cool words were heard trumpeted forth with the voice of a herald: 'Even if there had been a thousand navigators, they could not have hit it off to a hair like this in their reckoning; we are not a half mile off.' "

Their joy was short-lived. As they drew closer, they saw that the land was not at all similar to the region around Petropavlovsk. There was no sign of the three volcanic peaks, and what they had thought was the entrance of the bay proved to be the open sea between two overlapping islands. The sun came out at noon, giving them their first opportunity in ten days to make an observation, and they discovered they were in latitude 54° 30′, almost two degrees north of Avacha Bay. Still Khitrov insisted they were off the coast of Kamchatka, and when Steller expressed doubt he was reminded contemptuously: "You are not a sailor."

The wind freshened from the northeast toward evening, with occasional snow squalls, and they spent the night tacking to hold their position at a safe distance from land. The increasing gale forced them to carry full canvas in order to avoid being driven onto a lee shore. Dawn of the fifth revealed that the weakened shrouds of the mainmast had parted from the force of the wind and weight of the ice-covered sails. "We noticed that our two fore-braces had also parted," Waxell reported, "nor did we have anyone able to repair the damage with a knot or splice . . . we were more like a wreck than a ship."

At eight o'clock that morning Waxell and Khitrov called a sea council. All the petty officers and seamen who could drag themselves from their bunks gathered in Bering's cabin, a conclave of walking skeletons. Even to men in their own emaciated condition, the appearance of the Captain Commander came as a shock. His rotund face had caved in, the yellowed skin hanging from the cheekbones in loose folds. He had lost all his teeth; his lips barely met over the swollen gums, and his mouth was a black ruin. Since his sickness he had been unable to shave, and a matted beard covered his chin, not blond but white. His eyelids kept sagging, and he made an effort to focus on the silent circle around his cot.

Waxell opened the council with a resume of their critical situation: only six barrels of water in the hold, the mainmast unserviceable, the sails rotted and in tatters, not enough ablebodied men left to handle the ship in bad weather. Winter storms and snow were now upon them, and every hour's delay brought them nearer to disaster. Under the circumstances, he proposed that the *St. Peter* seek harbor in a bay which lay only six miles to the west.

Bering raised himself painfully to a sitting position. With his gaunt face and snowy beard, he resembled an Old Testament prophet. His voice was a hollow echo, and they had to bend their heads to hear him.

"We have already risked and endured worse than our present state," he pleaded. "We can still use the foremast, and there are yet some casks of water to see us the rest of the way. At least, we should make an attempt to bring the *St. Peter* back to Avacha Bay."

Khitrov was quick to refute him. They should think of their own lives, he argued, and trust to Providence to preserve the ship. Though the land to the west was obscured by clouds, he was convinced that it was a headland of Kamchatka. They would send to Lower Kamchatka Post for natives with dog-sleds to transport the sick men. The crew hesitated. Their instinct was to follow the Captain Commander "unless they could be assured that this land was Kamchatka," Steller's journal quoted them. "If it was not, they would be prepared still to risk the utmost and work to the last. . . . Master Khitrov assured them that, if this were not Kamchatka, he would let his head be cut off," and one by one they nodded in agreement.

Bering turned to his adjutant, Dmitri Ovtsin, and asked him to express his thoughts. Young Ovtsin had been a lieutenant in the Imperial Navy, and had surveyed the River Ob for the Kamchatkan Expedition; but through political enemies in St. Petersburg he had been demoted to the rank of ordinary seaman. His well-bred face was drawn with fatigue, and he licked his lips to speak. "It is our duty to safeguard Her Majesty's property —"

Khitrov's bellow of protest drowned the rest of Ovtsin's statement. "As he concurred in the opinion of the Captain Commander," Steller reported in his journal, "the order of both the officers was: 'Get out, hold your tongue, scoundrel, rascal!' and so he had to leave the council." Steller was called on last, "according to the favorite order of precedence," he observed sardonically, "but warned by the example of Ovtsin I answered: 'I have never been consulted from the beginning, nor will my advice be taken if it does not agree with what is wanted; besides, the gentlemen themselves say I am not a sailor; therefore I would rather not say anything.' "

Waxell and Khitrov had won the council's vote, and the crew filed out of the cabin. Bering settled back on his cot, and closed his eyes in resignation. He knew that he was dying, and his one wish was to be buried in home soil. Now he must lie in a lonely grave on an island without a name.

Their course was set WSW toward the bay, and the crew, once the decision had been made, collapsed in utter exhaustion. Even the instinct of self-preservation was not enough to keep them alert, and they lay in their bunks while the ship drifted closer and closer to shore. Steller's apprehension increased as neither Waxell nor Khitrov appeared on deck to take command. "When toward four o'clock in the evening we were so near land that it appeared to be scarcely four miles away from us, and for three hours no officer had shown himself, as was usual on all dangerous occasions, and all were gently and sweetly sleeping, I went to the Captain Commander and begged that he might order that at least one of the officers should remain at his watch in order to decide on the place to anchor, since it looked as though they were intending to run ashore without further precaution. Both officers were indeed ordered on deck, but they evinced no further concern than to order the course to be held straight for land."

Shortly after sunset they dropped anchor in twelve fathoms, in full view of a sandy beach with no apparent rocks or obstructions. The wind had gone down, and everything indicated a quiet night. Half an hour later, a surf began to run with the outgoing tide, and the vessel was tossed like a ball in the violent turbulence. Heavy seas snapped the anchor cable and swept them toward a reef, suddenly exposed by the low tide, over which the breakers were pounding and forming.

There was such confusion on board that "no one any longer knew who should give or should take orders. All that the officers, terrified and seized with the fear of death, did was to shout that a new anchor be thrown over into the surf." The second cable promptly parted, and the desperate sailors were about to let go their third and last anchor when former lieutenant Ovtsin, the only one to keep his head, warned them that it would be useless in the raging waters.

The *St. Peter* was in only five fathoms; twice her keel bumped on submerged rocks, and another heavy blow was certain to split her in twain. They had been carrying the bodies of two scurvy victims, in order to bury them ashore, but the superstitious seamen regarded the corpses as the cause of their peril, and "they were thrown without ceremony neck and heels into the sea." Men ran about aimlessly, wailing and screaming, and asking childish questions. One distracted sailor inquired of Steller "whether the water was very salty, as if death in fresh water would be more delightful. Another, for the better encouragement of the panic-stricken men, shouted: 'Oh, God! It is all over with us! Oh, God, our ship! A disaster has befallen our ship!' " Khitrov had gone into hiding while the danger lasted. "God now laid bare the resoluteness of the hearts which ordinarily were bursting with courage," Steller pointed out with grim satisfaction. "He who until now had been the greatest talker and advice-giver kept himself concealed, until others, with God's help, had found a way out, whereupon he began valiantly to preach courage to the men, though he himself from high-heartedness was as pale as a corpse."

At the last moment, as they were carried onto the reef, a huge wave lifted them up and over the rocky ledge, and they found themselves miraculously afloat "in a placid lake, all at once quiet and delivered of all fear of stranding." The sheet anchor was lowered in four and a half fathoms on a clean sandy bottom, and the battered hulk of the *St. Peter* came to rest, never to sail again.

The seas had subsided with the turning tide, and the ship rocked as gently as a cradle in the serene swells. A November moon was in its first quarter, and the pale wet light revealed a crescent of white beach less than half a mile away. Grass-covered dunes rolled inland toward a shadowy plateau at the base of the mountains, whose snow-covered summits glowed like phosphorus against the midnight sky. The bone-weary sailors had relaxed in deep slumber, and the sick men had ceased their moaning, comforted by the belief that they had reached Kamchatka and help was close at hand. Only Steller lay awake, troubled by grave misgivings.

VII. BERING ISLAND

LATER they realized how providential their escape had been. On each side of the little bay, shelving rocks extended a couple of miles out to sea. So narrow was the entrance between them that another hundred feet in either direction would have meant disaster. "We came to know of only one such passage that is free from ledges," Steller wrote, "and this is precisely the stretch to which, as, disheartened and in desperation, we were blindly sailing full tilt on to the land and to our doom, God in his wisdom and love directed us."

Actually the harbor was none too secure, protected from the ocean only at low tide when the reef was exposed. They woke on Friday to find the ship pitching and tossing again with the incoming flood; and it was not until noon that the feeble remnants of the crew could load the empty water casks and lower the longboat into the surf. Forty-nine men were down with scurvy now, twelve had died, and another score would succumb before the scourge ended.

Steller had spent the morning packing his specimens, for he could see from their perilous position that the first violent storm would either drive the *St. Peter* out to sea or dash it to pieces against the rocks. He and Plenisner and his servant Lepekhin boarded the longboat, together with Waxell and a few of the more critically ill. "We had not yet reached the beach when a strange and disquieting sight greeted us, as from the land a number of sea otter came toward us in the sea, which from a distance some of us took for bears, others for wolverines." When they stepped ashore, they were surrounded by hordes of blue foxes, who drew their lips back from their teeth in a snarl. Some animals ran at the visitors boldly and snapped at their legs, and the sailors had to drive them off with kicks. The fearlessness of the otters and foxes was proof to Steller that they had never seen man before.

Not far from the landing place they found a stream of clear water, which had not yet frozen over; but there were no trees or shrubs except the creeping Arctic willow, less than a foot high and the thickness of a finger. The only fuel was the driftwood on the beach, already partly covered by snow. While the watering party built a fire and endeavored to make the sick men comfortable, Steller and Plenisner set off to investigate their surroundings, returning toward evening to find Waxell very weak and faint. They refreshed themselves with tea, and Steller gave voice to the secret fear they all felt. "God only knows whether this is Kamchatka."

Waxell's lantern jaw set in stubborn lines. "What else can it be?" he demanded. "Help will be on the way soon. The ship we shall cause to be taken to the mouth of the Kamchatka River by cossacks, the anchors can be had any time, the most important thing now is to save the men."

Plenisner had killed a half dozen ptarmigan, and several of these were carried out to the *St. Peter* by Waxell that evening to be given to the Captain Commander, in the hope that fresh food might revive him. Steller added some nasturtium-like herbs and brooklime, both of which he knew possessed antiscorbutic properties. He prepared a soup out of the remaining ptarmigan, and gathered some more brooklime and nasturtiums for the scurvy patients who remained onshore. Plenisner made a shelter out of driftwood and a torn section of sail, and they slept that night alongside the sick.

Steller still doubted that they had reached the coast of Kamchatka; and the following morning, while Plenisner was hunting more ptarmigan, he and Lepekhin decided to explore further. The desolate beach echoed to the gloomy croak of ravens, and small flocks of sandpipers trotted along the edge of the flattening breakers, hunting for crustaceans left on the sand as the waves receded. Diminutive brown wrens, which the Russians call "little tobacco quid," scuttled like mice around the rocks, their thin shrill notes louder than the boom of the surf.

The shore grew increasingly rocky and narrow as they proceeded south; the steep mountains came almost to the sea, and a partly submerged reef ran parallel to shore. Several enormous dark-colored forms like overturned boats were drifting slowly along the reef, feeding underwater with only their backs exposed. Sometimes one would lift its snout and expel air with an explosive snort. Steller had never seen such creatures before, and he asked his cossack whether they could be sperm whales or possibly the giant sharks he had heard about in Kamchatka; but Lepekhin replied that they were quite unknown back home. His suspicion that they were not on the mainland was confirmed when he noticed, far to the west beyond the mountains, the grayish-blue reflection of the ocean on the low overcast, an Arctic phenomenon called "water-sky." Now he was convinced that "we were on an island surrounded by the open sea."

That night around the campfire he confided his conclusion to Plenisner. They could not count on an early escape, he said, and must face the probability that they would have to winter here. Since it would be suicidal to remain on the damaged vessel, he suggested "building a hut for all eventualities and assisting each other with word and deed as good friends, no matter how the circumstances might shape themselves." They sealed their pact with a handshake, and Steller added in his journal: "Although for appearance's sake, in order not to discourage me, he did not assent to my opinion that this was an island, nevertheless he accepted my plan in regard to the hut."

Young Thoma Lepekhin took the news hard, and his eyes filled with sudden tears. "He regarded me as the cause of his misfortune," Steller observed, "and reproached me for my curiosity which had led us into this misery, [thus] making the first step to our future companionship. 'Be of good cheer,' I said, 'God will help. Even if this is not our country, we have still hope of getting there; you will not starve; if you cannot work and wait on me, I will do it for you; I know your upright nature and what you have done for me; all that I have belongs to you also; only ask and I will divide with you equally.' "

Lepekhin was inconsolable. " 'Good enough; I will gladly serve Your Majesty, but you have brought me into this misery. Who compelled you to go with these people? Could you not have enjoyed the good times on the Bolshaya River?' "

His candor amused Steller, and he replied to the boy gently: " 'God be praised, we are both alive! If I have dragged you into this misery, you have in me, with God's help, a life-long friend and benefactor. My intentions were good, Thoma, so let yours be good also.' " He reminded him: " 'Moreoever, you do not know what might have happened to you at home.' "

The problem of winter quarters was solved ingeniously. Near the mouth of the stream they had noticed a number of deep pits dug in the sandy banks, the immemorial burrows of the blue foxes. By enlarging these dens, shoring them up with driftwood, and covering them with fox skins and the rotted sails of the *St. Peter*, shelters could be provided for all the crew; and, since the dwellings would be underground, they would have added protection from wind and storms. On the eighth, Khitrov arrived in the longboat with ten more scurvy patients and the body of Nils Jansen, the boatswain, who had died earlier that morning. While the boat crew was shoveling out the fox dens, the sick men and the corpse of the boatswain were placed in a circle around the little fire. Several times the sailors had to drop their work and drive off the ravenous foxes, who bit off the fingers and toes of the dead man and sniffed hungrily at the nostrils of the others to see if they were still breathing.

Bering was brought ashore on the afternoon of the ninth. So many of the sick had expired when they were taken from the putrid hold and exposed to the air that, as a precaution, the Captain Commander was covered with robes. Four men carried him up the beach in a litter made of two poles with ropes slung between, and placed him in a special pit under a tarpaulin. Steller, who spent the first night with him, "wondered at his composure and singular contentment." His courage in the face of death moved Steller deeply, and he regretted his earlier outbursts of temper. For the first time, he clasped the older man's outstretched hand and held it as Bering made an effort to speak. "What do you make of this land, Mr. Steller?"

"It does not look to me like Kamchatka, sir," Steller answered honestly. "The great number and tame assurance of the animals indicates that it must be sparsely populated or not at all."

The Captain Commander nodded, and his eyelids half-closed.

"Nevertheless I believe we are not too far from the mainland," Steller added. "Today I found buried in the sandy beach a poplar-wood shutter with cross moldings, undoubtedly of Russian workmanship. There was also what I took to be a fox trap with the teeth made of tusk shells, called *Dentalium*, which do not occur in Kamchatka. It may have been washed over from America."

Bering's mind seemed to wander. "The vessel can probably not be saved, may God at least spare our longboat."

The task of removing the rest of the stricken crew from the *St. Peter* proceeded slowly. Because of the rough seas it was impossible to row to and from the ship for days at a stretch, and deaths aboard became a routine entry in the log. The trumpeter Toroptsov, who had blown the mock salute for Steller, was lowered over the side on the eleventh. On the fourteenth, three sailors died as they were brought up on deck, and a fourth succumbed on the way to the beach. Steller was particularly grieved over the loss of "the old and experienced mate, Andreyan Hesselberg, who had served at sea for more than fifty years and at the age of seventy was discharging his duties always in such a way that he carried to his grave the reputation of a preeminently useful man, whose disregarded advice might perhaps have saved us earlier."

Conditions were not much better ashore. Driftwood for the underground huts had to be dragged a considerable distance, and the handful of men still able to work had not yet completed the shelters. The sick lay on the open beach under rags and bits of canvas, sometimes half buried by the drifting snow. When a man died, his comrades were too weak to remove the body, and it remained alongside the living. At night they could hear the foxes gnawing at the corpse.

"Everywhere on the shore there was nothing but pitiful and terrifying sights," Steller sympathized. "Some sick cried because they were so cold, others because hungry and thirsty, since the mouths of many were so miserably affected by the scurvy that they could not eat because of the great pain, as the gums were swollen like a sponge, brown-black, grown over the teeth and covering them." His previous contempt for his Russian shipmates was forgotten. Now, in their adversity, he worked tirelessly to minister to the needs of the crew, bringing them warm soups and antiscorbutic herbs and roots which he dug from the frozen ground.

Any lingering thought of an early rescue vanished when the gunner's mate, Boris Roselius, completed a five-day reconnaissance trip. Bering had ordered him to take two men and proceed in a northwesterly direction along the coast in search of forests or signs of human habitation. Roselius returned on the fifteenth to report that he had found no paths or fireplaces or other indication that human beings had ever set foot on these shores. Now the marooned sailors realized there was no one to help them. Their chances of survival depended on themselves.

Fresh food was the first concern; and that afternoon Steller, with Plenisner and assistant surgeon Betge, went a couple of miles down the beach to hunt for sea otters. They crept up on a pod of unsuspecting animals, clubbed four who were sleeping on the rocks, and brought them back to camp. From the liver, kidneys, and heart they made what Steller called "several palatable dishes," though he admitted that the others "wondered at my taste, which adapted itself to circumstances."

A young, still suckling otter was roasted and given to the Captain Commander, but he showed "a very great disgust" at the rank-smelling flesh, and refused it despite Steller's plea that it had high medicinal content. The meat was divided up among the crew, and the priceless pelts, which would have brought a year's wages in Siberia, were tossed aside to spoil or be chewed to bits by the foxes.

The castaways had adopted a new set of values. Money was worthless here; a pouchful of rubles could not buy a driftwood log, a jeweled finger ring was not so precious as a handful of rye flour. Ordinary items which they would normally have scorned to pick up — rusty nails, bits of twine, the broken handle of an axe — were hoarded as rare treasures. Steller could see a deeper change. "We all realized that rank, learning, and other distinctions would be of no advantage in the future or suffice as a means of sustenance."

Strict shipboard discipline had yielded to a more informal relationship. Officers no longer gave orders, and ordinary seamen were addressed politely by their patronymics, the Russian method of acknowledging a person of equal or superior rank. "We soon learned that Peter Maximovich was more ready to serve than Petrusha was formerly." Both officers and sailors knew that their salvation depended on mutual consideration and mutual respect, and all decisions were made by common consent. Food was rationed equally, and men of all ranks were divided into work groups and assigned particular tasks: some to finish the huts; some to evacuate the remaining crew and supplies from the *St. Peter;* some to gather firewood; some, like Steller, to stay at camp, doing the cooking and tending the patients and making harnesses to haul driftwood over the winter.

The first two underground shelters were completed by mid-November, and the sick were moved into the larger, nicknamed "the Barracks." Space was limited, and they lay shoulder to shoulder on the packed sand, so crowded that one man could not shift position unless the others turned over at the same time. Next to it was the hut occupied by Steller, Plenisner, Betge, gunner's mate Roselius, and guard-marine Boris Sint — "we five Germans," Steller called them proudly — as well as Lepekhin and two other cossacks. In front of each dwelling stood several barrels which served as storehouses for keeping their supply of meat from the ubiquitous foxes, and they erected scaffolds upon which to hang clothing out of reach.

Day and night the foxes swarmed like flies over the campsite, attracted from miles around by the scent of food, and their audacity and cunning made them a constant nuisance. Nothing was safe against their thievery, nothing frightened them away. Steller with an axe "killed over seventy in three hours," he recorded, but the rest became all the more aggressive. "They crowded into our dwellings and stole everything they could carry away, including articles that were of no use to them, like knives, sticks, bags, shoes, socks, caps. . . . While skinning animals it often happened that we stabbed two or three with our knives because they wanted to tear the meat from our hands. However well we might bury something and weight it down with stones, they not only found it but, like human beings, pushed the stones away with their shoulders. If we cached something up in the air, they undermined the post so that it had to fall down. We always slept with clubs in hand so that when they waked us we could drive them away or knock them down."

The voracious pests mutilated the bodies of the dead before they were interred, or dug them up from their fresh graves. They preyed on the helpless sick, tearing the clothes from them and chewing the leather soles of their boots. Even the well were molested. "One night when a sailor on his knees wanted to urinate out of the door of the hut, a fox snapped at the exposed part and, in spite of his cries, did not soon want to let go. No one could relieve himself without a stick in his hand, and they immediately ate up the excrement as eagerly as pigs."

Harassed beyond endurance, the sailors took childish revenge on their tormenters. "Inasmuch as they left us no rest by day or night we became so embittered against them that we killed young and old, did them all possible harm, and tortured them most cruelly. . . . Every morning we dragged by their tails for execution before the Barracks our prisoners who had been captured alive, where some were beheaded, others had their legs broken or one leg and the tail hacked off. Of some we gouged out the eyes; others were strung up alive in pairs by their feet so they would bite each other to death. Some were singed, others flogged to death with the cat-o'-nine-tails. Nevertheless they would not be warned and keep away from our huts; and finally countless numbers could be seen running about without a tail or on two or three legs."

Waxell was the last to leave the *St. Peter*. As long as the ship was at sea, he had fought the scurvy and forced himself to keep moving; but no sooner had they anchored than he collapsed, and his limbs became so stiff that he could not move without the assistance of two men propping him up by the arms. "I had not become badly ill until I took up my quarters in the galley," he recalled. "It was possible to keep a small fire burning there, and I had assumed it would be more comfortable . . . but the bad air and filth found its way from the hold where so many had been lying ill for two or even three months, attending to the needs of nature where they lay. I suffered so severely from this evil, unhealthy stench that I became unable to use either my feet, hands, or my teeth, and so was as good as ready to be claimed by death."

There were still seventeen men aboard, most of them confined to their bunks, and five corpses. On the nineteenth, Waxell discovered that only four buckets of fresh water were left, and he hoisted a red flag in the main shrouds and an empty water cask at the trysail gaff and fired several cannon as a distress signal. Unfortunately the onshore wind was so strong that the longboat could not row out to him, and he was forced to gather up some snow which had fallen during the night and melt it for drinking water. It was not until November 21 that the wind subsided sufficiently for the longboat to come alongside, and the crew tossed the corpses overboard and evacuated the sick men.

Waxell seemed more dead than alive. His face was sunken, the large features standing out like the ridges of a skull, and his tawny beard was matted and caked with blood. As they were carrying him from the galley to the deck, he fainted three times. He was placed in the Barracks with the others, until a separate shelter could be prepared for him. "He was so ravaged by the scurvy that we abandoned all hope for his life," Steller related, "but nevertheless we did not fail to come to his help with both food and medicine . . . as it was feared that, after his decease, when the supreme command would fall to Khitrov, the universal hatred would delay, or even prevent, the enterprises necessary for our deliverance."

Khitrov was likewise a victim of scurvy — though Steller claimed "he was mostly sick from laziness" — and had been laid in the sandpit with the rest of the patients. He implored the five Germans to take him into their dugout "and give him a corner, because he could not possibly longer remain among the crew, who day and night let him hear reproaches and threats for past doings, but as our dwelling was already filled up and as nobody was allowed to undertake anything without the assent of the others, all of us objected, as all were equally insulted by him, and refused him absolutely." Khitrov was left in the Barracks, where "nothing was heard but wailing and lamenting, the men times out of number calling down God's judgment for revenge on the authors of their misfortunes."

Before abandoning the *St. Peter*, everything possible had been done to make her secure. In addition to the sheet anchor, Waxell had dropped a kedge and grapnel, and struck the yards and topmasts. Bering recommended that the vessel should be hauled up on shore and made fast with hawsers, and assigned the task to Khitrov; but there were only four able-bodied men available, and Khitrov protested he was so ill "that he could not leave the tent for any reason." On the night of November 28, a week after the last survivors had been brought off, a violent northeasterly storm broke the weakened cables and threw the *St. Peter* high and dry on the beach near the dugout camp. She lay on her beam ends in her final resting place, her rudder lost and the port side stove in below the waterline. The strong ebb and flow of the tide lowered her eight or nine feet into the loose sand, burying her up to her wales, and gradually the wreck filled with salt water and silt. Men climbed the slanting decks to salvage what foodstuffs they could from the flooded hold, their footsteps unnaturally loud in the eerie stillness below.

Bering's death closely followed the loss of his ship. He had no more will to live. His own life was wrecked; he blamed himself for the catastrophe which had befallen his expedition, and his only concern was the rescue of the crew. In the final order of his career, on December first, he dispatched another scouting party south "to examine the shore and to determine if they were on an island or not." Though he was convinced by now that they had not reached Kamchatka, he kept his opinion to himself so that he would not dishearten the others.

Each day he grew progressively weaker, and Steller could do nothing to revive him. He was worn out in body and spirit, his once rugged constitution had been undermined by scurvy, and he was "almost eaten up by lice." The fluid which had caused the swelling of his feet extended to his abdomen and chest, and a rectal fistula appeared which, as soon as it was opened, forced gas gangrene into the tissues, resulting in excruciating pain.

Recollections of the past ten years flashed through his tortured mind: the heartbreaking six-thousand-mile trek across Siberia, the constant harassment by the Academy, the refusal of the Admiralty to give him proper authority, the endless frustrations and disappointments and delays which had led to this final disaster. He had tried to carry out his assigned duty, but at his advanced age his strength had not been equal to the extra burdens imposed on him. Now he awaited the end "with calmness and earnest preparation for his passing, which came while he was in full possession of his reason and speech."

His bed was a little depression in the floor of his underground shelter, and the loose sand sifted between the uprights and trickled down the sides into the hollow. Bit by bit it covered his feet, then his legs, and finally his thighs, until he lay half-buried like the hulk of the *St. Peter*. When Steller sought to remove the sand, the Captain Commander opened his eyes and his voice seemed to come from very far away. "Let me be," he murmured. "The deeper in the ground I lie, the warmer I am; only the part of me that is above ground suffers from the cold." He died two hours before daylight on December eighth, and his body had to be exhumed in order to give him decent burial.

"A righteous and devout Christian," Steller called him,

"whose conduct was that of a man of good manners, kind, quiet, and universally liked by the whole command both high and low." Too late, he recognized the Captain Commander as a gentle and just leader whose sole fault was that he was "too lenient" with his jealous subordinates, and "was not born to quick decisions and swift action; however, in view of his fidelity, dispassionate temper, and circumspect deliberateness, the question remains whether another with more fire and heat would have overcome equally well the innumerable obstacles to his task."

Despite the tragic fate of the *St. Peter*, despite subsequent Russian efforts to disparage its Danish captain and claim credit for themselves, historians rank Bering today with Columbus and Cook among the great explorers of all time: "The illustrious commander of the expeditions which disclosed the separation of the two worlds and discovered north-westernmost America."

He was buried, with the rites of the Lutheran Church, on a hill overlooking the beach and his wrecked ship. "His corpse was tied fast to a plank," Waxell wrote, "and thrust down into the ground." A crude wooden cross was erected over the grave, and the island was given Bering's name.

VIII. THE LONG WINTER

CHRISTMAS DAY was cold and raw, a penetrating chill which cut to the marrow. Three more crewmen had succumbed to scurvy earlier in December, and the others, racked by hunger and pain, huddled their emaciated bodies close together for warmth in the dank underground burrows. Snow covered the beach before the camp to a depth of several feet by now, and they could not find enough wood to keep a steady fire going. Winter gales tore savagely at their shelters and ripped off the canvas roofs, and the sick lay under the leaden sky with only their rags to protect them from the elements.

There was not much for a Christmas feast: sea otter meat, cormorants, blue foxes. The rye flour and groats which they had salvaged from the *St. Peter* had been "lying pressed hard into leather sacks for two or three years and, after the stranding of the ship, had been impregnated with substances dissolved in the salt water, particularly gunpowder," Steller noted in his journal, "to such a degree that in eating it one did not dare consult one's taste. Until we got used to it, our bodies became distended like drums from flatulence." They had no ovens to bake bread, but they mixed the flour with warm water in a wooden dish and let it ferment and turn sour, and "small cakes were fried from it in the Russian manner with seal fat."

On Christmas night toasts were drunk with tea made of cranberry and wintergreen leaves dug from the snow, and Steller's fine tenor voice led his companions in the old *Weihnachtslieder* he had learned as a choirboy in Bavaria. The sound of carols defied the lonely rumble of surf and the wailing wind, and those who could walk or crawl gathered outside the hut in the darkness and joined the singing, German and Scandinavian and Russian accents mingling in the universal language of Christmas, and for a few hours they imagined themselves "in other places where everything was in abundance."

Slowly, almost imperceptibly, the influence of Bering had worked a profound change in Steller. In his grief at the death of the Captain Commander, he seemed to inherit some of Bering's own qualities of patience and understanding, and he displayed a new tolerance toward the helpless Russian crew. As a doctor, it was natural for him to aid the sick; and his early religious training made him a source of spiritual strength. During their ordeal he was indefatigable and devoted, sharing his own food with the sufferers or staying awake all night to ease the last moments of a stricken sailor. Waxell's earlier dislike of the quick-tempered young scientist yielded to open admiration for the way that "he exhorted them to patience and steadfastness in their misery and comforted the dying."

Some still clung to the forlorn hope that they were on a peninsula of Kamchatka, or at least that there might be human habitation. The three-man scouting party, which Bering had dispatched on December first to explore the coast to the south, had not been heard from since; and the castaways took this to be an encouraging sign. Perhaps the party had stumbled on a native settlement, perhaps even now help was on its way. Their hope was dashed when the scouts returned the day after Christmas, after wandering for almost four weeks across the desolate snow-covered interior in freezing weather without shelter or adequate food. Although it had been impossible to follow the coast because of the rugged mountains, they reported, they had no doubt that this was a deserted island. There was only one note of optimism: they had found so many fragments of oars, Kamchatkan rudders, and bottoms of fish barrels washed up on the beach that they were convinced, like Steller, that the mainland could not be far away.

A month earlier, such discouraging news might have broken the spirit of the marooned crew; now they felt almost a sense of relief at learning the worst. The mood of dark depression was lifting. Fresh meat and wholesome water and the bulbs and roots gathered by Steller were showing their effects, and the scurvy epidemic had been checked. Early in January of 1742 the plague claimed its final victim, petty officer Lagunov, bringing the total of deaths to thirty-one out of a crew of seventy-seven. The sick were slowly regaining their strength, many could stand again and walk without support, and their teeth grew firm enough to chew the tough and sinewy otter flesh. They revived more rapidly toward the end of the month "when our company killed the first sea lion," Steller

recorded. "The meat was found to be of such exceptional quality and taste that we only wished soon to get hold of more.
The fat was like beef marrow, and the meat almost like veal."

As their morale improved, the castaways looked to the future with new confidence. Waxell, who had succeeded Bering
as supreme commander, was still gravely ill, but he forced
himself to set an example for the crew. "We young men kept
our courage up," he wrote, "resisted with firmness all discour-
agement, made it a duty to still enjoy life and to make as much
as we could out of our prison home."

On January 18 he called a council of all forty-six survivors "to consider how we were to escape from this wretched
spot." Each individual was urged to voice his opinion "so that
we might unanimously choose the best of all the different
views. I explained to them that our plight was the same for
one and all, and that the lowliest seaman longed for deliverance just as much as the first officer; therefore, we should all
stand by each other as one man. If we did what lay in our
power to do, God would give it His blessing, for He helps all
who help themselves."

Various ideas were advanced at the council. Some suggested covering the longboat with a deck of sailcloth to make
it fit for an ocean voyage, and sending it due west with a crew
of five or six to carry news of their disaster to Kamchatka and
arrange for a rescue vessel. Waxell did not reject this recommendation out of hand, and even admitted he might agree to it
if nothing better could be devised; but he warned that the
small boat would not be able to weather a severe williwaw and
"would incontestably founder, and all on board would be lost.
Those left behind on the island would live in constant anxiety
and doubt, as they would have no means of knowing whether

the boat had succeeded in reaching Kamchatka or not, and meanwhile no further steps would be undertaken . . . in working for our deliverance." Even if the boat made Avacha Bay, he added, the supply ship might have left for Okhotsk, and the castaways would have to wait over another winter here and face death by starvation, since the sea animals were becoming increasingly shy and might in time quit the island altogether.

Others proposed that an attempt should be made to move the *St. Peter* into deep water and sail her home. Waxell replied that the vessel was sunk so deep in the sand that it would require far more men than they had to free her. "We would also need numerous logs for rollers," he pointed out, "of which we do not possess even one. Furthermore, we know that the bottom of the vessel is damaged, for the level of water in her hold is the same as that of the sea, and rises and falls with the tide. Nor is it possible to dig a canal out to sea, because the bottom is quicksand and what we might dig out at low tide would fill up again with sand at the next flood, and we could thus go on digging for all eternity without making any progress."

His own suggestion, backed by Khitrov, was to dismantle the *St. Peter* and get sufficient timber from her to build another vessel capable of carrying everyone. This proposal was vigorously opposed by former Lieutenant Ovtsin, whose demotion in rank had left him with an abiding fear of the authorities in St. Petersburg. His thin refined face wore an expression of shocked concern. "It would be an unwarrantable action to break up one of her Imperial Majesty's ships," he protested. "We should expose ourselves to well-deserved punishment if we destroyed government property without permission."

As before, Khitrov shouted him down and ordered him to

leave the council; but Waxell silenced the Fleet Master with a terse command. He put his suggestion to a vote, and "it was agreed (Ovtsin dissenting) that in the spring the *St. Peter* should be broken up and out of the wreck some kind of smaller vessel should be made to take us to Kamchatka."

A formal statement to this effect was drawn up and signed by everyone but Ovtsin. "I wanted this document," Waxell confided in his memoirs, "because . . . if we did not succeed, I did not want the entire blame heaped on myself, and so I felt that such a precaution was called for. She [the *St. Peter*] was a very stoutly-built ship, well put together with iron and nails, and I could not foretell what would be the outcome of breaking her up. If things were to go wrong, I anticipated that there would be as many proposals as heads, and that I should be told that if only we had acted on this or that, it would have been all right. In such a situation, I would not have been sure of my life."

Now there was nothing to do but wait for spring, and the stranded crew set up their camp routine to operate more efficiently during the long months ahead. The occupants of each dugout were organized into units, whose members hunted and cooked and gathered firewood together. Waxell and his officers shared the labor with the men, "for our situation was no respector of persons," he stated, "and it was with us, as it stands written, that he who will not work shall not eat." Their supply of grain was so short that he "could only allot to each man thirty pounds of rye-flour a month, later reduced to fifteen pounds and finally to nothing, and also five pounds of wet groats and half a pound of salt. When spring came, we were all to try and live off plants and wild roots, so that we might keep 800 pounds of rye-flour for our voyage away from the island, if God should help us to leave. Everybody was satisfied . . . that we all, the high as well as the low, should enjoy the same ration without consideration of person or rank."

Each man was issued his own axe, knife, pots, and pans, as well as needles and cobbler's tools in order to repair torn clothing or worn-out footgear. Dress overcoats were made over into work blouses, knapsacks fashioned into boots, leather provision sacks cut into soles. "Since nobody would work for money," Steller observed, "everyone had to act as shoemaker, tailor, glover, butcher, carpenter, cook, and footman as best he could, so that henceforth they would have been able to earn an ample living in all these trades." Tobacco was the only item of barter, and Steller, who did not enjoy smoking, paid his scientific assistants for their services with his allotment of coarse shag, and with pipestems which he made from the wing bones of young black albatrosses.

In spite of the effort at equality, the more educated few continued to direct the rest. Steller's household had taken in the two cossack servants of the late Captain Commander, and thus was evenly divided, five Germans and five Russians. They were separated into shifts of one German and one Russian each, and assigned particular tasks. "We thus had the advantage that we [Germans] did not have to build fires, fetch water, nor open or close the chimney. Furthermore, after meals, the kitchen and table utensils were rinsed and put away by them, in return for which they received from us kettles, dishes, plates, spoons, tablecloths, and other effects. . . . Everyone knew at all times his duty and business without having to be reminded of it. This arrangement made all labor bearable and resulted in cheerfulness and good feeling among us and in our having greater abundance of better prepared food and drink than in any of the other households. At the same time everybody was permitted, when we deliberated about something, to express his opinion and the best advice was taken without respect of persons."

Now winter closed in with its brief gray days and interminable nights. Although the temperature never dropped as low as zero, and generally hovered in the middle twenties, the average humidity was eighty-six per cent, and the dampness and fog rotted the sails that covered the burrows until they could no longer withstand the Arctic storms. Banshee winds screeched through the narrow valleys between the mountains, the terror of the sound enhanced by the reverberating thunder of breakers on the rocky shore. Occasional gusts were so severe that "people getting out of their hollows to answer nature were whirled away," Waxell related, "and would undoubtedly have been blown out to sea had they not flung themselves on the ground and clung to a stone . . . lying there until the worst was over."

In February a sharp earthquake shook the camp, preceded by what Steller described as "a strong subterranean wind which seemed to proceed with violent hissing and roaring from south to north and which became stronger the nearer it approached us." The weak supports of the huts buckled, and the loose sand walls collapsed onto the sick and covered them completely. Only the prompt action of their comrades saved them from being suffocated. While the tremor continued on land, Steller was puzzled to note, he "could not observe the slightest unusual motion in the sea."

Firewood was getting harder and harder to find, and sometimes the castaways were forced to eat their food raw. When they first arrived, the men could gather enough on the beach in front of the camp; but by February they had to search ten or fifteen miles north and south along the shore. The driftwood lay buried under as much as six feet of snow, and they would look for a telltale hummock in the flat surface, and dig as eagerly as treasure-hunters in hopes of uncovering a log or baulk, more precious than gold. The bundles of fuel were hauled back to camp by means of yokes worn across the breast, tied with ropes.

By rare luck, late in the month, a party of wood-gatherers discovered a dead whale washed up on the beach, only five miles away. "Its blubber was slightly rank," Waxell admitted, "for it must have been drifting about the sea for some considerable time; but we were highly satisfied with that piece of good fortune and called the whale our provision store. When we were unable to get other sea creatures, we could always have recourse to it." The blubber was cut into small squares and boiled in water "so that the liquid train-oil should run out. The remains, consisting of nerves and sinews, we swallowed bit by bit without chewing. It was easy to get the pieces down as we were never able to get all the oil out of them."

Any change was a welcome relief from the steady diet of sea otter, which most of the sailors found repugnant. In addition to its offensive flavor, the leathery meat had to be "chewed, chewed, and chewed again" before it was soft enough to be swallowed; but it was virtually their only source of food, and hunting parties prowled the shore day and night, armed with long driftwood poles. If they sighted an otter sleeping on the rocks, one man would creep toward him, keeping as much as possible against the wind, while the others cut off his passage to the sea. As soon as the quarry was within striking range, Steller wrote, the hunter "sprang up suddenly and tried to beat him to death with repeated strokes on the head. However, if he ran away before he could be reached, the other men together chased him from the sea farther inland and gradually closed in on him, whereupon, no matter how nimbly and adroitly the animal might be able to run, he would finally fall into our hands exhausted."

Despite the urgent need for meat, Steller's observant eye was making mental notes of the otters' habits, to be expanded in his manuscript later. "If they have the luck to escape, they begin, as soon as they are in the water, to mock their pursuers in such a manner that one cannot look on without particular pleasure. Now they stand upright in the water like a man and jump up and down with the waves and sometimes hold the forefoot above the eyes as if they wanted to scrutinize you closely in the sun; now they throw themselves on their backs and with the front feet rub the belly and the pudenda as do monkeys; then they toss the young ones into the air and catch them again, etc. If a sea otter is overtaken and sees nowhere any escape it blows and hisses like an angry cat. When struck it prepares itself for death by turning on the side, draws up the hind feet, and covers the eyes with the forefeet. When dead it lies like a person, with the front feet crossed over the breast."

Lately the sea otters had been growing scarcer. At the outset they could be seen in large herds anywhere in the vicinity of the camp, playing or sleeping along the beach in complete security; but as the hunting continued they became more wary. Before swimming ashore, they would stand erect in the water and scan the beach cautiously, turning their noses in all directions to catch any suspicious scent. Even when they settled down to rest on the rocks, they remained tense and nervous, jumping up again in fright at the least sound and scrambling back to sea. Each herd posted a lookout to alert the others in case of danger, and the ever-present foxes helped thwart the hunters by barking a warning. The parties were compelled to search constantly for new grounds, farther and farther from camp. Before the winter was half over, the otters had been driven entirely from the eastern side of the island by men "raging among the animals without discipline or order," Steller protested, "for the purpose of sacrificing the skins to their covetousness and gambling passion."

Bored by the monotony of their dreary existence, the castaways had turned to gambling to while away the long dark months. Packs of cards were salvaged from the wreck of the *St. Peter*, and the sailors spent their idle hours squatting on the floors of their dugouts, playing for otter pelts as stakes. They had been brutalized by the years of hardship in Siberia and by their tragic voyage, and had grown callous and insensitive to killing; but Steller, a dedicated naturalist, was outraged at the pointless butchery, and his strict religious code disapproved of gambling.

"The scurvy had barely subsided when a new and worse epidemic appeared," he wrote in his journal. "I mean the wretched gambling with cards, when through whole days and nights nothing but card playing was to be seen in the dwellings, at first for money, now held in low esteem, and, when this was gambled away, the fine sea otters had to offer up their costly skins. In the morning, at inspection, no other topic of conversation was heard than: this one has won a hundred rubles or more, and that one has lost so and so much. He who had totally ruined himself tried to recoup his losses through the poor sea otters, which were slaughtered without necessity and consideration only for their skins, their meat being thrown away. When this did not suffice, some began to steal the skins from the others, whereby hate, quarrels, and strife were disseminated through all the quarters."

Steller made formal complaint to Waxell and Khitrov, though he suspected that the Fleet Master was profiting privately from the gambling and acquiring a stock of valuable pelts to bring home for sale. Waxell refused to intervene; he knew the temper of the crew, and felt that this was no time to exert his authority. "Severity would be quite useless," he explained to Steller. "Shipboard discipline has ended, the officers are hopelessly outnumbered, and the only way to control the men is with the greatest possible mildness and calmness."

"But card playing by sailors is forbidden in the Imperial Navy," Steller remonstrated.

"The ukase against playing cards was issued without any thought of shipwreck on a desert island, Mr. Steller. If the Admiralty had had any inkling of our pitiable circumstances, I am sure they would have introduced a special paragraph giving permission for such a pastime. Far from forbidding those under my command to play cards, I am glad they have found something with which to pass the time and help them to overcome the melancholy from which most of them suffer badly."

Their restlessness increased with the first promise of spring. The snow had settled and packed hard, storms were less frequent, and March turned out to be surprisingly sunny and warm. They still hoped against hope that a neck of land might link them with Kamchatka, and scouting parties set out on further reconnaissance trips, traveling up and down the coast until impassable mountains blocked their way. One group led by boatswain Alexei Ivanov returned on March 8 from a four-day exploration, reporting that they had been halted by steep rocks extending into the sea, but bringing the welcome news that the first fur seals had arrived on the southern beaches, all of them old males who customarily precede the females to the rookeries. Ivanov was sent out again on March 22, with instructions to "go across or along the mountains and keep on until he came to some mainland or to the end of the island." Steller accompanied him partway, his first journey across the island, and in a bay on the Kamchatka side he discovered a large number of sea otters, still "feeling secure and lying together in herds, so that we could have killed probably a hundred had we not thought more of the meat and general welfare than of the precious skins."

The island was so narrow that the new hunting grounds were only twelve miles from camp, but the trail over the mountains was toilsome and hazardous because of sudden blizzards. "Three times there happened such disastrous accidents on this trail that almost a third of our men might have been lost." On April first, gunner's mate Roselius, assistant surgeon Betge, guard-marine Sint and a cossack left their dugout to hunt the new sea otter grounds which Steller had discovered on the opposite coast. That evening a violent northwest storm struck, with winds so strong that they could not stand upright or see a step ahead. Six feet of snow fell during the night, and in the morning they could barely dig themselves out and flounder through the drifts to the beach. Steller and the other members of the household had just finished breaking out the entrance to their hut when three of the hunting party made their way back to camp, "out of their minds and unable to speak, as stiff as machines, and the assistant surgeon quite blind. We undressed them at once, covered them with feather beds, and revived them with tea." An hour later the guard-marine was found in a still more pitiable condition, wandering aimlessly on the beach. During the night he had fallen into a brook, his clothing and limbs were frozen almost solid, and it was feared he would lose his hands and feet. His strong constitution pulled him through, but Betge did not regain the use of his eyes until eight days later.

Undismayed by this near disaster, Steller set out on April 5 in search of meat for the camp, accompanied by Plenisner and Thoma Lepekhin and one of Bering's servants whom he had adopted. The weather was pleasant and sunshiny, and they killed as many otters as they could carry back, and built a campfire beside a cliff to wait till morning. Toward midnight another northwest storm "brought so much snow that, since we could not get under shelter, the cossack soon lay buried covered deep without moving, while I sat in the snow and by constantly smoking tobacco tried to keep myself warm and banish the thought of death." Plenisner and the servant kept running back and forth during the night, despite the difficulty of keeping on their feet in the gale. "As day broke, though hardly to be distinguished from the darkest night, and as my other companions would not let me rest under the snow, I finally got up in order to search for a crevice in the rocks. . . . My cossack, who, when I spoke to him, would not get up, we dug out of the snow by force." They separated into two parties to look for cover, and young Lepekhin "after half an hour's search found a very wide and spacious cave in a cliff which without doubt had been caused by a great earthquake."

They followed Lepekhin to the cave, carrying wood and meat, and made themselves comfortable, safe at last from snow and wind. Adjoining it was a smaller cave "in which we could keep our supplies safe from the thieving foxes, and even a chimney formed by Nature, through which the smoke found an outlet through the cracks in the rock without in the least annoying us in our quarters, which became properly heated from the fire. Here we spent, with hearts very thankful to Providence, three days in hunting, as the foxes had devoured our provisions during the storm." They returned to camp on April 8 "with much booty and good news to our people, who were already fearing that we would never appear again." Steller added with pride: "The cave, as well as the bay, were afterwards named for me," but his name never appeared on any official Russian chart.

Second mate Yushin, who had led a small group on a hunting expedition about the same time, had an even closer brush with death. Forced by the storm to seek shelter, they had taken refuge in a fold of the cliff close to the ocean. High tides kept them imprisoned there for seven days, standing on a narrow ledge with the water up to their ankles. They linked arms and slept in shifts, each man held up by his comrades to keep him from toppling forward. The sea did not subside until the eighth day, and they straggled back to camp half dead from hunger and exhaustion. On one point all the hunting parties agreed: they were definitely on an island, and their only escape was by water.

Now that their last doubts were resolved, Waxell called another ship's council on April 9, which unanimously reaffirmed their previous decision to build a smaller vessel, since the *St. Peter* was "not fit for further sea service," the log stated. It was arranged that "twelve men skilled in the use of the axe should work continuously on the carpenter work." All the others, with the exception of Lieutenant Waxell and Fleet Master Khitrov and Doctor Steller, as he was now respectfully called, were detailed under Yushin's leadership "to hunt and to supply the camp with meat. Whatever they got should be divided equally among all according to the size of each group." When a party returned from a hunt, the men would be given a day's rest, after which "they should attend to the housework and mend clothing and shoes and assist with the work on the vessel, until their turn to hunt came around again."

The actual work of breaking up the wreck was delayed, since the following day was Palm Sunday, and the sailors refused to perform any labor during Holy Week. On Easter Sunday, April 18, a party of hunters killed the first fur seal, an old bull weighing over seven hundred pounds. They were overjoyed at this stroke of luck, and calculated that the carcass would supply them with food for a week. Unfortunately, even the iron-stomached Steller conceded that the meat "smelled like fresh white hellebore, thereby became repulsive to the taste, and in the case of many of the men induced violent vomiting with diarrhea." Later he found that the flesh of the females and younger seals was more palatable and, when roasted, tasted like young pig. It became his favorite dish while on the island.

The sea provided other bounties. A sea lion, which had been wounded in Kamchatka with a harpoon, was discovered on the beach, dead but not yet spoiled. "The most delicate part of this animal is the flippers," Steller noted. "When boiled they swell up a great deal and can then be easily skinned." As a further boon, a "quite fresh whale" was cast ashore less than three miles away, furnishing so much blubber and oil that several barrels remained untouched when they departed.

On the day after Easter the dismantling of the old ship began. Everything useful had been removed from the vessel and piled on the beach above high water. "Grindstones were dressed and placed in troughs, tools were cleaned of rust and sharpened, a smithy erected, crowbars, iron wedges, and large hammers forged, driftwood gathered, and charcoal made." Carpenters clambered over the empty hulk, ripping out planks and joists like a swarm of foxes tearing at a corpse. Everything was haunted by memories of the past: the wheelhouse where Waxell had steered the ship into the giant wave, the broken supports of the gunport bulwark that had been swept over the side, the narrow cot in which the Captain Commander had lain for so many months. The pounding hammers were the ghostly tread of footsteps on the bridge, the screech of a pulled nail was a scream of pain echoing from the hold.

Within a couple of weeks they had done what the ocean could never do. Decks which had withstood the battering of the sea yielded to prying crowbars. The stout foremast which had not snapped in the fiercest williwaw was chopped down with ease by a handful of men. The *St. Peter* had carried them over five thousand miles of the North Pacific; now it was reduced to a heap of splintered timbers.

Waxell looked on in silence. His lanky frame was bowed with the weight of his new responsibility, and his tawny beard showed premature flecks of gray. Had he made the right decision to destroy the old ship? Could they build another vessel as staunch? He was coming to know, as Bering knew, the loneliness of command.

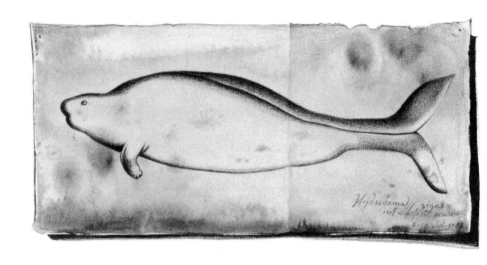

IX. STELLER'S SEA COW

SPRING ARRIVED with a rush of wings. Suddenly the April
sky was filled with migratory birds, returning to their
northern nesting grounds on Bering Island. Murres and kittiwakes stirred the slumbering shores to life. The long-silent
hills resounded to the harsh laughter of red-throated loons
and the low liquid notes of the dainty snow bunting, its familiar melody carrying Steller back to his boyhood days in Windsheim.

The drifts were still deep in the valleys when the first red-
footed black guillemots came in from the sea, and settled on
the rocky ledges of their old rookeries. White-breasted auks
followed them, whistling shrilly from the cliffs behind the
camp. Here and there, where the snow had melted on the
slopes, Lapland longspurs chirped their pessimistic refrain,
brooding over the past days of gloom and fog, and were answered by the wildly joyous song of skylarks which heralded
the end of the long winter.

Day and night the V-shaped skeins of wild geese wove their cobwebby patterns across the sky, baying like packs of hounds as they swept overhead. Ducks in countless numbers, mallards and pintails and shovelers and teal, stooled in to join the graceful harlequins which remain on Bering Island year round. Immense rafts of bright eiders rocked on the ocean, half a mile from shore; they too had wintered here, but soon would head farther north to breed in the highest Arctic latitudes. Their color was generally white, Steller observed, with brown underparts as though they had skidded through the mud. They were extremely shy and flew at terrific speed, outdistancing any other duck, and he was unable to collect a specimen. Later Pallas named the species Steller's Eider, *Polysticta stelleri*, in honor of the first naturalist to record and describe it.

All winter the ptarmigan had lived peacefully together, but with the coming of spring the flocks disbanded, and every bare spot on the tundra became the scene of a battle royal among the cocks. Their neck feathers had turned russet, in contrast to their pure white bodies, and fiery red combs swelled above their eyes. While the hens looked on, barely visible against the snow, the cocks spread their wings and rushed at each other, buffeting and pecking and spurring with their feet. Their throats rattled like snare drums as they leapt to meet their rivals, sometimes springing ten or fifteen feet in the air in a blizzard of scattered feathers.

The pestiferous blue foxes had withdrawn to the hills for the mating season, and the nights were loud with their snarling and howling. "They stink much worse than the red foxes," Steller noted. "In rutting time they buck day and night, and bite each other cruelly for jealousy. Copulation itself takes place amid much caterwauling like cats." The marooned men were grateful for a respite, however brief, from their incessant thievery and depredations.

The milder weather brought other benefits. As the snow receded on the beach, the castaways discovered large quantities of driftwood which had been hidden all winter, and the task of making charcoal for the smithy became much easier. Palatable herbs sent up their first tender shoots, and under Steller's direction the men dug medicinal plants from the tundra: Kamchatkan sweet grass, whose root resembles the parsnip and is as edible as the stalks; the delectable bulb of the Sarana lily; sea lungwort, brooklime, and bitter cress, all of which gave new strength to their scurvy-depleted bodies. Now Waxell realized his mistake in not listening earlier to Steller, whom he acknowledged to be "a great botanist and anatomist, well versed in natural science." The health of the sailors was not fully restored until they ate the fresh greens he recommended.

Spring was not an unmitigated blessing. The snow which was packed deep in the narrow valleys began to thaw rapidly, and the southeast wind brought heavy rains which turned already swollen brooks into foaming torrents. The stream beside camp rose over its banks, inundating the flat land near the mouth, and the underground burrows were flooded with as much as two feet of water. The men were forced to abandon their dugouts, and all work on the *St. Peter* was halted until they could build new shelters on sloping ground to provide drainage.

They had been making substantial progress in dismantling the wreck, and by the end of April they were ready to begin on the new craft. All three of the ship's regular carpenters had died of scurvy; but fortunately Waxell discovered among the survivors a Siberian cossack who had formerly been employed as a laborer when the packet-boats were being built at Okhotsk. The cossack assured Waxell that "if I would give him the proportions of the new ship he would build it under my guidance and make her so solid that, with God's help, we should be able to put to sea in her." His assistance was of such value that he was subsequently appointed a Siberian nobleman on Waxell's recommendation.

On May 5 the keel of the new vessel was laid, and the stem and stern posts erected. That afternoon Waxell invited the whole command to be his guests, "making everybody bring their own beaker or something out of which to drink, for my service did not consist of much." They celebrated with a Siberian drink called *saturnan* or tea soup, usually made of good butter and fine wheaten flour, over which the tea is poured until the mixture becomes as thick as chocolate. "Not having any of these ingredients, I used train-oil, musty rye-flour, and crakeberry plants instead of tea. I prepared a portion that entirely filled our large ship's-copper. They all drank with good appetite and became quite gay and cheerful, without anyone becoming intoxicated, and thus we spent the rest of the day right until midnight."

During May and June, while the beach before the camp echoed to the busy sound of saws and hammers, Steller spent his time exploring the island more extensively, compiling field notes on the local flora and fauna. He had made himself a stout pair of mukluks out of sealskin, and a coat of the black skins of newborn fur seals, and carried his writing paper and quill pen and inkpot in a waterproof pouch fashioned of seal intestines. With young Lepekhin, he wandered over the alpine meadows, bright with wild roses and violets and golden-flowered rhododendron. He was amazed at the luxuriant vegetation which had sprung up like magic on the bare hills, stimulated by the long hours of arctic daylight; in some places he came upon almost impenetrable thickets of blackberry and salmonberry bushes six feet high. Anemone and purple fireweed dotted the lower slopes, and the wet sphagnum bogs were white with the bloom of cloudberries. Altogether he listed 211 varieties of plants, most of which were also to be found in eastern Siberia and in the mountain regions of Europe.

The birds on Bering Island were likewise similar to those of Kamchatka, with three notable exceptions. One was a "white sea raven . . . impossible to reach because it only alights singly on the cliffs facing the sea"; it has never been identified or seen again. Another was "a special sea eagle with white head and tail. In the highest rocks overhanging the sea, it constructs a nest of two ells [about five feet] in diameter, composed of twigs gathered from a great distance, and strewed with grass in the center, in which are one or two eggs, in form, magnitude, and whiteness very like those of a swan. At the beginning of June they have young ones that are completely covered with white down." His discovery is known today as Steller's Sea Eagle, one of the three American eagles, so rare that only two have been spotted in Alaska since Steller's time, and ornithologists suspect that the species has become extinct.

The third he described as "a special kind of large sea raven with a callow white ring around the eyes and red skin about the beak, which is never seen in Kamchatka, and occurs only on the rocks near Steller's Cave." The Spectacled Cormorant, one of Steller's most sensational finds, was flightless like a penguin, its stubby wings too small to lift its heavy body, and so helpless that within a hundred years it was totally exterminated by ruthless hunting. This ungainly survivor of prehistoric times was as large as a goose, weighing up to fourteen pounds, "so that one single bird was sufficient for three starving men." Steller prepared it by encasing the bird, feathers and all, in a mold of clay, and baking it in a heated pit to make it tender. In spite of the fact that the spectacled cormorants were extremely plentiful — Steller called them "copiosissimi" — there are only six mounted specimens in existence today, and collectors prize it more highly than the great auk.

On the side of the island facing Kamchatka, countless herds of fur seals and sea lions "covered the whole beach to such an extent that it was not possible to pass without danger to life and limb." The great rookeries had never been disturbed by man, and Steller had a unique opportunity to study the animals in their natural state. He chose a slight elevation in the center of the rookery, and built a flimsy blind of driftwood. Here he remained concealed for six consecutive days, surrounded on all sides by an undulating gray ocean of massive bodies, slumbering or fighting or scratching themselves lazily with the long flexible fingers on their hind feet. His ears rang with the deafening chorus of babies bleating like lambs, the mothers whinnying in a higher register, here and there a ferocious old bull — called *sikatch* or beachmaster — bellowing his deep bass challenge to anyone who might dare raid his harem. "If I were asked to state how many I have seen on Bering Island," he estimated conservatively, "I can say without lying that it is impossible to make any computation. They are innumerable."

Crouched in his blind, his writing pad balanced on a knee, Steller composed on the spot the definitive chapter on fur seals, which covers fourteen pages in his famous monograph *De bestiis marinis*, published by the St. Petersburg Academy ten years after his death. He even dissected and analyzed the outer and inner structure of a large bull, his detailed measurements and anatomical observations occupying another thirteen pages. So thorough and accurate was his account, written under impossibly difficult conditions, that when the United States took possession of the Pribilof Islands a century later, the government experts who surveyed the fur seal herds could make no corrections or changes in Steller's classic description.

In painstaking Latin he recorded the complete life history of this hitherto little-known species: the first appearance of the fat sullen bulls a full month before the rest of the herd; their bloody battles for possession of the females, forming harems containing as many as fifty cows; the black wide-eyed pups which were born shortly after the females came ashore and had to be nursed for weeks on land until they learned to swim. He marveled at the ability of each mother to pick out her own baby among the hundreds of thousands of youngsters playing along the beach. Most incredible of all, he noted that the big *sikatches* never reentered the sea after their arrival on the island, taking neither food nor water for three months, until they were weak and lean as skeletons at the summer's end.

While in Kamchatka, Steller had learned that the fur seals traveled north from the Kurile Islands each spring and gathered off the coast of Kamchatka, disappearing suddenly in June and showing up again toward the end of August on their way back south. Native hunters had told him that most of the seals they killed in the early summer were females heavy with young, and also noted that the males were exceedingly thin when they returned in the fall. From this information Steller concluded that Bering Island was their summer breeding ground, and he was all the more convinced that the mainland must be somewhere close by.

Although the hunting parties went out daily in search of meat for the camp, there was never a sufficient supply on hand. All the remaining otters had been driven to the opposite coast of the island, and the parties had to detour around the seal rookeries and make a thirty-mile round trip over the mountains, increasingly arduous since by now many of them were barefoot. The carpenters building the new vessel complained to Waxell that they did not have enough to eat, and asked his permission to hunt the sea animals themselves. Waxell knew that the ship might not be completed before the September storms if they halted work now; and he cast longing eyes at an abundant supply of fresh food which drifted tantalizingly under their very noses, just offshore.

Ever since the stranding of the *St. Peter*, the hungry crew had watched these strange monsters, which the Russians called sea cows, come close to the beach with each flood tide to crop on the pastures of seaweed; but the creatures weighed several tons, and scurvy had left the sailors too feeble to capture one. Now necessity spurred them to action. On May 21, an attempt was made to hook a sea cow from shore with a large iron gaff, fastened to a heavy line, but their quarry snapped the hawser with ease and escaped out to sea. After several more efforts had failed, they decided to resort to the native method of harpooning.

The ship's boat, which had been damaged on the rocks in the autumn, was repaired, and they fashioned a fifteen-pound iron hook, "the point of which somewhat resembled the fluke of an anchor," Steller related, "the other end being fastened by means of an iron ring to a very long and stout rope, held by thirty men on shore. A strong sailor took this hook and with four or five other men stepped into the boat, and one of them taking the rudder, the other three or four rowing, they quietly hurried toward the herd. The harpooner stood in the bow of the boat with the hook in his hand and struck as soon as he was near enough, whereupon the men on shore pulled the desperately resisting animal laboriously towards them. Those in the boat made the animal fast by means of another rope and wore it out with continual blows, until, tired and completely motionless, it was attacked with bayonets, knives and other weapons and pulled up on land. Immense slices were cut from the still living animal, but all it did was shake its tail furiously and make such resistance with its forelimbs that big strips of the cuticle were torn off. In addition it breathed heavily, as if sighing. From the wounds in the back the blood spurted upward like a fountain. As long as the head was under water no blood flowed, but as soon as it raised the head up to breathe the blood gushed forth anew."

Harpooning a sea cow could be a hazardous business. "When an animal caught with the hook began to move about somewhat violently, those nearest in the herd began to stir also and feel the urge to bring succor. To this end some of them tried to upset the boat with their backs, while others pressed down the rope and endeavored to break it, or strove to remove the hook from the wound in the back by blows of their tail, in which they actually succeeded several times. It is a most remarkable proof of their conjugal affection that the male, after having tried with all his might, although in vain, to free the female caught by the hook, and in spite of the beating we gave him, nevertheless followed her to shore, and that several times, even after she was dead, he shot unexpectedly up to her like a speeding arrow. Early next morning, when we came to cut up the meat and bring it to the dugout, we found the male again standing by the female, and the same I observed once more on the third day when I went there myself for the sole purpose of examining the intestines."

To the half-starved castaways, the sea cows were like manna from heaven. "We now found ourselves so abundantly supplied with food that we could continue the building of our new vessel without hindrance," Steller rejoiced. He spoke eloquently of the superlative quality of the flesh. The fat, which covered the body to a thickness of four inches, was "glandular, firm, and shiny white, but when exposed to the sun takes on a yellowish tinge like May butter. Both the smell and the taste of it are most delicious, and it is beyond comparison with the fat of any marine animal, and even greatly preferable to the meat of any quadruped, since in addition it will keep ever so long even during the hottest days without becoming rancid or strong-smelling. Melted, it tastes so sweet and delicious that we lost all desire for butter. In taste it comes pretty close to the oil of sweet almonds. . . . The meat, when cooked, although it must boil rather long, is exceedingly savory and cannot be distinguished easily from beef. The fat of the calves is so much like fresh lard that it is hard to tell them apart, but their meat differs in no wise from veal." He found that the muscles of the abdomen, back and sides, when preserved in salt, "became so seasoned that they are in every respect equal to corned beef and most delicious. The internal organs, heart, liver and kidneys are too hard and were not in great demand by us, as we had the greatest superabundance of meat."

Even the new supply of available food — Waxell stated that one sea cow gave enough to last the entire company for a fortnight — was not so important to Steller as the opportunity to examine more closely these fabulous animals, which until now he had only seen half-submerged along the reef. The northern manatee, or Steller's Sea Cow, was a separate species found only in the area around Bering Island and adjacent regions of the North Pacific. It belonged to the Sirenian order of mammals, a group which includes the dugong and southern manatee and which is believed by some to be descended from land animals ancestral to the elephant. "To the navel it resembles a land animal," he noted; "from there on to the tail, a fish." It measured from twenty-eight to thirty-five feet in length and twenty-five feet in girth, and weighed up to four tons. The corrugated outer skin was blackish-brown, full of grooves and wrinkles, and the head suggested "in some measure a buffalo head, particularly as concerns the lips." Instead of teeth, it masticated its food like a bovine with the horny plates of its gums. Steller's description of this long-extinct creature, more than any other achievement, has made his name immortal. No complete skeleton or skin has survived. All that science knows of it today is the chapter in *De bestiis marinis*, written on Bering Island over two hundred years ago by the only naturalist who ever saw the sea cow alive:

"Every day for ten months during our ill-fated adventure I had a chance to watch from the door of my hut the behavior and habits of these creatures. . . . With the rising tide they came in so close to the shore that not only did I on many occasions prod them with a pole, but sometimes even stroked their backs with my hand. If badly hurt they did nothing more than move farther away from shore, but after a little while they forgot their injury and came back. Usually entire families keep together . . . to me they appear to be monogamous. They bring forth their young at all seasons, generally however in autumn, judging from the many newborn seen at that time; from the fact that I observed them to mate preferably in the early spring, I conclude that the fetus remains in the uterus more than a year. That they do not bear more than one calf I conclude from the shortness of the uterine cornua and the dual number of mammae, nor have I ever seen more than one calf about each cow.

"These gluttonous animals eat incessantly, and because of their enormous voracity keep their heads always under water with but slight concern for their life and security, so that one may pass in the very midst of them in a boat and single out from the herd the one he wishes to hook. All they do while feeding is to lift the nostrils every four or five minutes out of the water, blowing out air and a little water with a noise like that of a horse snorting. While browsing they move slowly forward, one foot after the other, and in this manner half swim, half walk like cattle grazing. Half the body is always out of the water. Gulls are in the habit of sitting on the backs of the feeding animals, feasting on the vermin infesting the skin. . . . Where they have been staying even for a single day, there may be seen immense heaps of roots and stems. Some of them when their bellies are full go to sleep lying on their backs, first moving some distance away from shore so as not to be left on dry land by the outgoing tide.

"In the spring they mate like human beings, particularly towards evening when the sea is calm. Before they come together many amorous preludes take place. The female, constantly followed by the male, swims leisurely to and fro, eluding him with many gyrations and meanderings, until, impatient of further delay, she turns on her back as though exhausted and coerced, whereupon the male, rushing violently upon her, pays the tribute of his passion, and both give themselves over in mutual embrace."

Steller was determined to complete his description of the sea cow by analyzing its inner structure and anatomy. A large female had been caught and hauled ashore; and on July 12, a climactic moment in his career, he set about the herculean task of dissecting the mammoth carcass on the beach. According to his estimate, it weighed about 8000 pounds; the heart alone tipped the scales at 36¼ pounds. The stomach was "of amazing size, 6 feet long, 5 feet wide, and so stuffed with food and seaweed that four strong men with a rope attached could scarcely move it from its place and drag it out." It had to be cut because "it could not be taken out whole, with the liver, on account of its great size."

Since the emancipated sailors could no longer be ordered to aid him, he hired assistants and paid them in tobacco, which had taken the place of money. The indifferent helpers soon tired of their work and "from ignorance and disgust would tear everything to pieces, and acted according to their own inclinations; in addition I had to express satisfaction, in spite of the loss and damage caused by them, in order that they might not desert me altogether. Not a single gut could I get out entire, nor unfold it when gotten out." The incompetent assistants were not Steller's only problem. The weather was rainy and cold, the observations could be made only in the open and at certain stages of the tide, and "packs of most despicable Arctic foxes were tearing with their vile teeth and stealing everything from under my very hands, carrying off my paper, books and inkstand while I examined the animal, and ripping it while I was writing."

Despite the difficulties, he did not resort to field notes, but wrote down in concise Latin every anatomical detail, precisely as it was to appear in his monograph: "The eyes of this animal, in spite of its size are not larger than sheep's eyes, [and are] without eyelids. The ears are so small and hidden that they cannot at all be found until the skin has been taken off, when its polished blackness reveals the ear opening, hardly enough for the insertion of a pea. . . . The feet consist of two joints, the extreme end of which has a rather close resemblance to a horse's hoof, and I hesitate whether to call them hands or feet for the reason that with the exception of the birds we do not have a single two-footed animal. With these front feet, on which neither fingers nor nails can be distinguished, the animal swims ahead, knocks the seaweed from the rocks on the bottom, and, when lying on its back getting ready for mating, one embraces the other as with arms.

"Under these forefeet are found the breasts, with black, wrinkled, two-inch long teats, at the end of which innumerable milk ducts open. When pulled hard these ducts give off a great amount of milk, which surpasses the milk of land animals in sweetness and richness. . . . The belly is roundish and very distended and at all times stuffed so full that at the slightest wound the entrails at once protrude with much whistling. . . . From the genitals on, the body suddenly decreases in circumference. The tail itself becomes gradually thinner toward the flipper, which serves as hind feet [and] is horizontal as in the whale and the porpoise." He added with keen perception: "From the head of their manati the Spaniards are said to take out a stone-hard bone. This I have vainly searched for in so many animals that I have come to think our sea cow may be a different kind."

Under his direction, the draftsman Plenisner made six accurate drawings to scale, which accompanied Steller's manuscript when it was sent to St. Petersburg. The illustrations disappeared en route across Siberia, and have never been found.

X. RETURN OF THE ST. PETER

B Y July their little vessel had begun to take shape. It was voted to christen her the *St. Peter* and dedicate her to the apostle as before. The superstitious crew feared that the patron of the old *St. Peter* would be offended if they gave the new ship another name.

She was rigged as a one-masted hooker with mainyard and mainsail, 41 feet from stem to sternpost and 36 feet along the keel, 11 feet in beam, and 5¼ feet deep. "For the keel," Waxell stated, "we used the old ship's mainmast which we sawed off three feet above the deck, not having either the tools or the strength to get it right out. The remaining stump of the mainmast had to serve as the new vessel's prow; the sternpost we made from a capstan which we had had on the old ship; the main-topmast, a large topsail-yard, the topgallant-mast and the jib-outrigger we were luckily able to transfer from the old to the new. All the rest was sawn up into 1½-inch planks, including the fore-mast and the remaining yards."

They had planned to cover the vessel with whole planks from keel to wales, but as lumber ran out they were forced to use some of the worn deck-planks to finish her. Inside, she was lined with the more damaged boards, full of nail holes and splintered and cracked from being wrenched loose; they were fixed to each rib with iron spikes, and helped to make the vessel solid. Deck-beams and a deck were laid, each beam well bolted to a knee timber. A small master's cabin was located aft, and forward was a galley where food for the entire company could be prepared. As the work progressed and hope of escape from their desert island mounted, the spirit of the crew rose markedly, and Steller, in a generous mood, gave particular credit to Waxell for his "constant efforts and friendly encouragement."

The planking was finished in late July, and the vessel was ready to be caulked and sealed. "There was no lack of hemp and old rope for caulking," Waxell wrote, "but we were extremely short of pitch with which to paint it over. To supply this want we adopted the following expedient: I had a quantity of anchor-rope that had never been in the water and this I cut up into pieces of a foot or less in length. I then unravelled the strands and put the whole thing into a large copper kettle" which was placed on a bed of coals. The slow heat tried out the tar with which the rope was impregnated, and "I obtained as much as I needed for the underpart of the ship. The seams above the wales, however, I was forced to grease with tallow."

Now the castaways were busy day and night, eager to leave before the dreaded autumn weather closed in. Ovens were constructed and bread was baked for the voyage; several barrels of sea cow meat were salted down; the broken water casks were repaired with makeshift hoops of rope. Half-inch planks were sawn out of two reserve anchor-stocks of birchwood, and a small jollyboat was built which could be carried on deck while the longboat was towed behind. Some dragged the bottom of the bay in a vain search for the *St. Peter*'s lost sheet-anchor. Others set to work on the sliding bilge-block from which the new vessel would be launched, a formidable task, since the ship had been put together high on the beach above floodtide and the distance to the water was 175 feet. Driftwood logs had to be hauled from the farthest part of the shore to build the ways, which were weighted with heavy cannon.

It was obvious that the little vessel could not hold all the spare items which had been salvaged from the wreck. Inasmuch as these were the property of Her Imperial Majesty's government, Waxell felt himself accountable for them. Rather than assume full responsibility, he called a ship's council on August first to debate whether he should assign part of the crew to remain behind and protect the surplus material, or take all the men and leave the goods unguarded. Since no one relished the thought of another winter in this desolate spot, it was unanimously agreed to build a *magazin* and store the material until it could be brought off at a later date. Khitrov made a complete inventory for the Admiralty and was careful to assure them that the goods would be safe because the island was "uninhabited."

On Sunday, August 8, all was in readiness for the launching at the first high tide. That noon the entire company assembled to hold divine services, and Lutherans and Russian Orthodox knelt side by side on the beach and offered devout prayers for a successful voyage. In the late afternoon, when the tide was at full flood, they started the vessel down the ways. To their consternation, the platform buckled under her weight and the hull landed with a heavy jolt on the sand. They worked all night to lift the vessel with makeshift jacks and place more planks under her, but it was not until full tide the following afternoon that the *St. Peter* could be launched, and anchored in three fathoms.

In the evening Waxell gave a reception to the crew, treating his guests to *saturnin* and fresh salmon which had been netted in the stream beside the camp. "Half the men were with me," he explained, "the other half in the ship taking advantage of the calm weather to step the mast and get up the rigging. Nor did we let our celebration last very long, for I thought: 'It is well to dry hay while the sun shines.'" They had in fact reached the most critical moment of the whole undertaking. The *St. Peter* was lying in the open water of the bay, "where for halfway round the compass, from NNW to SSE, there was not the least protection. If an onshore wind of any strength should get up, the ship would be driven on land and possibly destroyed."

The men labored around the clock to complete the rigging. Sails were bent on, the rudder hung, blocks and other naval stores taken aboard, and everything made clear to put to sea. Ten casks of fresh water, five barrels of sea cow meat, and eleven sacks of flour were stored in the hold, since there was no telling how long it might take them to reach Avacha Bay. The loading was completed on the morning of August 12, and at noon the crew brought out their baggage in the longboat.

Waxell had realized that there would not be room for all the bales of valuable sea otter pelts with which the men hoped to be "repaid in some measure for our sufferings." The total baggage limit was set at three and a half tons, and guard-marine Sint was charged with apportioning the weight to be allowed each member of the expedition, according to rank. Steller's allowance was fixed at 360 pounds, only half that of Waxell and 72 pounds less than Khitrov; and his protests were long and loud. At infinite pains, he had prepared a specimen of a young sea cow, consisting of a skin filled with dried grass and a complete skeleton — an item which would be beyond price today — and similar mounts of a sea otter and fur seal and sea lion. In spite of his coaxing and storming, he was told that there was no space for the specimens on the crowded ship, and he was not even permitted to bring small sections with him as samples. All he salvaged out of a whole year's collecting, beside his manuscripts, were the dried seeds of some American and Bering Island plants and a pair of the horny masticatory plates which served the sea cow instead of teeth. These palatal plates are now in the Museum of the Leningrad Academy of Sciences, the only ones in the world.

Miraculously there had not been the least breath of wind during the three days that the *St. Peter* lay vulnerable in the bay. Early on Friday the thirteenth the men left their huts for the last time "with much inner emotion," and boarded the vessel; and at six in the morning they weighed anchor. "We warped her through 4, 5, 7, and 9 fathoms of water," Waxell recorded, "and then took to our sweeps and rowed, with God's assistance, away from the island." By eleven o'clock they were outside the reef; a favorable wind sprang up, sails were hoisted, and they set course to clear the southeastern cape of Bering Island.

The crew stood at the rail as they pulled away from the deserted camp where they had spent more than eight desolate months. Already the foxes were ransacking their dwellings, devouring any scraps of meat or fat they could find, and Steller could see them tearing and ripping apart the mounted specimens he had been forced to leave behind. No one knew what fate was in store for them. No one could guess whether the vessel they had built "was going to bring us back to our beloved country, or to decide the outcome of our pilgrimage after so much toil, hope, and longing according to the will of the Almighty."

Slowly the shore receded, and the noon sun lighted a lone wooden cross on the hill behind the camp. Steller watched until it was lost in the distance. "The grace and mercy of God became evident to all," he wrote solemnly, "the more particularly when considering in what miserable condition we came to this barren island in November, how wonderfully we were fed, and how in spite of astounding toil we steadily gained in health and became more and more hardened and strengthened; and the more we gazed at it in parting the plainer appeared to us, as in a mirror, God's wonderful and loving guidance."

Not until they were all together on the vessel did they realize how cramped the quarters were. Waxell and Khitrov and Steller shared the single cabin aft, barely able to move amid the stacks of sea otter skins and personal effects. The other forty-three men occupied the twenty-foot hold, which was so crammed with supplies and water casks that there was not enough room to lie down. The crew was divided into three watches, and two sleeping places were assigned to three men. Still the space was too narrow, and they discarded everything they could spare, tossing bedding and sea pillows and clothing over the side. Even the black coat of newborn fur seals, of which Steller had been so proud, joined the long trail of debris bobbing on the waves in their wake.

The *St. Peter* rounded the cape safely, and sailed through the passage between Bering and Copper islands. "This afternoon was enjoyed very much," Steller entered in his journal on the thirteenth, "as in the clear and pleasant weather we coasted along the island, on which we knew every mountain and valley, which with much toil we had climbed so often in search of food or on some other reconnaissance." Swarms of sea birds rose and circled against the sky, and he could make out the seal rookeries and the faroff cliffs which hid Steller's Cave. Even Fleet Master Khitrov was unusually affable. "In a few short days," he assured everyone, "we shall drop our anchor in Avacha Bay."

They were delighted with the behavior of the little hooker. She responded well to the rudder, and could not have sailed better if she had been designed by a professional shipbuilder. Khitrov's log noted a couple of inches of water in the hold, but this was to be expected with new planking, and no one was concerned. By the following noon, they were eight nautical miles below the southernmost tip of the island, where so many sea cows were observed along the shore that they named it Cape Manati — a name it bears to this day — and Khitrov began his reckonings from this point. Toward evening the sea grew calmer, and by morning of the fifteenth the wind had all but died. The officers decided to cut adrift the longboat which they had been towing, since it was hindering the progress of the vessel. Relieved of her burden, the *St. Peter* picked up speed, and the last headland of Bering Island fell below the horizon.

That night they noticed that the water in the hold was increasing, and they kept a pump going constantly. The level continued to rise; they pressed their second pump into service, but both pumps soon clogged with chips which had been left by the workmen. At midnight they formed two bucket brigades and began to bail with pots and kettles from either hatchway. Still the level rose faster than they could bail. The wind was freshening, and pounding waves added to their danger. Panic spread among the sailors in the hold, now knee-deep in sloshing water; the longboat had been abandoned, the jollyboat at best could carry eight men, and there would be no escape for the others if the *St. Peter* foundered. Had they come all this way, they asked, only to drown almost within sight of home?

In their terror they turned to the officers for guidance, and the discipline which had collapsed during the long months ashore was suddenly restored. Waxell gave instructions to jettison the three cannon and several hundred pounds of cannonballs and grapeshot which they were carrying for ballast. When the sluggish ship failed to respond, he ordered the crew to throw overboard all the extra bales of sea otter skins. Too frightened to protest, the sailors reluctantly consigned the precious furs to the sea, and watched their hard-won fortunes sink from sight in the heaving waves.

As the hold was cleared and the hooker lightened, the cossack carpenter was able to locate the leak, just below water line. Several planks had spread, because of the strain on the frame when the *St. Peter* had to be jacked up during the launching. Rags and bits of clothing failed to caulk the gap, and in desperation the men sacrificed their remaining otter pelts to be cut into strips and stuffed between the planks. Wooden cleats were nailed over the priceless caulking, and the leak was arrested, though they had to keep bailing for the rest of the voyage.

On the seventeenth, about 9:30 in the morning, they sighted a snow-capped peak in the west, which Waxell identified as one of the high volcanoes near the mouth of the Kamchatka River. The weather was so thick and foggy that they did not close the mainland until they were less than a mile offshore, and they tacked to port and headed south. Under the lee of Kamchatka, they encountered sheltered seas and a dead calm, and nine more days were spent tacking and working their way slowly down the coast. At last, impatient at the delay, they manned the sweeps and advanced at the average rate of a quarter of a knot. On the night of August 26, after twenty-four hours on the oars without a break, they came opposite Vaua Point and the lighthouse which Bering had erected, and rowed past the Three Brothers into the entrance of Avacha Bay. At two o'clock in the afternoon of Friday the twenty-seventh — fourteen days after leaving Bering Island — the *St. Peter* dropped anchor in the inner harbor.

Some Kamchadals in *baidars* paddled out to the vessel, and brought the weary voyagers their first news of the outside world in fifteen months. It was depressing news: everyone had given up Bering and his crew for lost, the natives reported, and all the belongings they had left in Petropavlovsk had been sold or carried away by strangers. "Therefore, in a few seconds joy turned to anxiety in the hearts of all of us," Steller wrote in his journal. "However, we were all by this time so much used to misery and sorrow that, instead of looking forward anew, we only thought of continuing the old life and regarded the present circumstances as in a dream."

The *St. Paul* had returned safely to Avacha Bay last fall, they learned, when they went ashore, and Chirikov had been hailed as the discoverer of Bolshaya Zemlya. Bering, a foreigner, was completely discredited, and in the final appraisal all the honors were given to his Russian rival, though Chirikov had never sighted the mainland. "And thus having discovered the American coast 36 hours earlier than Bering," the historian Sokolof boasted with nationalistic pride, "and 11 degrees of longitude farther to the east, Chirikov returned to Kamchatka, having made on his route the same discoveries of the Aleutian Islands. . . . How different were the results, and what proof do they not furnish of the superiority of the Russians in scientific navigation!" And the French astonomer Delisle, whose faulty maps had been responsible in large part for their disaster, wrote disparagingly that Bering "sailed from Kamchatka, but did not go far, having been compelled by a storm to anchor at a desert island where he and most of his companions perished."

Not all the news that awaited them was bad. The demoted Lieutenant Ovtsin was informed that a ukase had been issued in St. Petersburg in February of 1741, too late to reach him before the expedition sailed, restoring him to his former rank in the Imperial Navy. Actually he had been the company's senior ranking officer under the Captain Commander. In view of his strong feelings against dismantling the old *St. Peter*, it is interesting to speculate what the fate of the survivors might have been had he assumed command on Bering's death.

On Saturday morning, led by Ovtsin, the survivors gathered in the little church at Petropavlovsk for a service of thanksgiving to "Almighty God for his gracious protection and their wonderful preservation." Later the sailors fulfilled the promise they had made at Bering's request during their storm-tossed voyage, and donated their last savings to cover the ikon of St. Peter with a casing of pure silver, bearing the inscription: "This holy obraz is adorned with a covering in accordance with the vow by Fleet-Lieutenant Dmitri Ovtsin and the entire service for being delivered from a barren island and reaching the Kamchatkan shore in the year 1742, month of August." According to local records, the silverwork was executed by de la Croyere's former repairman, the Immoral Clockmaker.

Waxell paused in Petropavlovsk to repair the damaged hull of the *St. Peter* in order to sail her to Okhotsk, but Steller was anxious to be separated from the crew as soon as possible. Their close comradeship, born of adversity during the shipwreck, had ended with their rescue; now the common danger was over, and once more he regarded his coarse Russian companions as little better than barbarians. On August 27 he arranged for his meager possessions to follow by winter sled, and with the faithful cossack Lepekhin he set out on foot across the peninsula to Bolsheretsk, to resume his scientific studies in Kamchatka.

Only Fleet Master Khitrov profited from the tragic voyage. Unknown even to Waxell, he had secreted a stack of prime pelts under his bunk when the order was given to throw them overboard. He smuggled the skins ashore, to be sold at a fabulous price to the Chinese, and babbled to everyone of the great numbers of sea otters to be found on Bering Island and the Aleutians.

The word spread quickly, and commercial fur hunters looked to the east with covetous eyes.

XI. JOURNEY'S END

THERE HAD been portentous changes in St. Petersburg during their absence. The Empress Anna, sponsor of Bering's voyage, had died in 1740, shortly after they left Okhotsk, and her two-months-old grandnephew Ivan had been designated as successor to the throne. A year later Elizabeth, shrewd and ambitious daughter of Peter the Great, had arrested the royal family in a palace coup, and proclaimed herself empress. Unlike her progressive father, Elizabeth had no interest in the westernization of her empire; all further efforts at exploration and expansion were curtailed, foreigners were looked on with suspicion, and Russia reverted to a policy of sullen isolationism.

Waxell had sailed from Avacha Bay on September 2, a few days after Steller's departure, but encountered such violent gales that he was forced to turn back and winter at Petropavlovsk. In the spring of 1743 the *St. Peter*, recaulked and her hull reinforced with one-inch birch planks, set out again, rounded Cape Lopatka safely, and reached Okhotsk on the twenty-seventh of June. That fall Waxell and his crew joined Captain Chirikov, now senior officer of the expedition, at his Siberian headquarters in Yeniseisk. The ailing Chirikov was still awaiting orders to return to St. Petersburg, but the Empress Elizabeth was not concerned with the fate of her father's enterprise. It was not until 1745 that the long-delayed dispatch arrived and Chirikov departed for home, leaving Waxell in supreme command of the expeditionary forces in Siberia.

It took the bureaucrats on the Neva six years to order Waxell back. His recall was issued in 1748, just before Chirikov's death, and he arrived in St. Petersburg with the last survivors in January of 1749, bringing the expedition officially to an end. A quarter-century had elapsed since Peter the Great had issued his instructions to Bering to explore the mysteries of the North Pacific, and the results of the long voyage were pigeonholed and ignored in the new isolationist atmosphere of the capital. Waxell was eventually promoted to captain second rank, but Khitrov, being Russian, fared better. Having taken full credit to himself for the rescue of the castaways, he was awarded the rank of rear admiral in 1753.

Steller never returned to St. Petersburg. Upon his arrival in Bolsheretsk, he decided to remain in Kamchatka, a voluntary exile without plan or future. He had no desire to face the intrigues of the Russian capital. In the wave of hostility toward all foreigners which marked the Empress Elizabeth's reign, his German associates at the Imperial Academy of Science had found life so unbearable that most of them had fled the city. Those who remained were afraid to voice any opinion at variance with the despotic government, lest they be consigned to the dreaded slave camps of Siberia; and Steller, who was well aware of his own hot temper and chronic inability to hold his tongue, realized he would be safer here in the Kamchatkan wilderness than among the spies and informers of Elizabeth's court.

In November of 1742 he dispatched a lengthy report to Gmelin at the Academy, apologizing for his failure to "accomplish something worth while" on the expedition, and laying the blame on "the lazy and pompous conduct of the officers Waxell and Khitrov." He expressed particular regret that he was "not able to bring to Kamchatka my collections, rare skeletons, and skins," but declared, with the devotion of a true scientist, that in spite of the losses and hardships "I would not exchange the knowledge of nature which I acquired on this rotten voyage for great wealth."

He sent another letter to St. Petersburg in November, addressed to his wife. During the lonely months on Bering Island, he had thought of the young and hot-blooded Brigitte with increasing longing. Her refusal to accompany him on his mission was forgiven, and he was willing to overlook the gossip of her gambling escapades and flirtations in court society. Their lengthy separation had rekindled his old desire, and he wrote her affectionately that he "wished nothing more than to see her again." Her reply, received at Bolsheretsk the following spring, expressed no joy at his safe return, but complained that the annual payment of two hundred rubles had not been received for two years, and she had been forced to sell his cherished library of natural history books to meet her expenses. Steller never referred to Brigitte again, save for a bitter paragraph in his *Pro Memoria*, written shortly before his death, which stated that "my effects must not be placed at the disposal of my wife . . . she should be satisfied with her allotment."

That winter Steller earned his keep by teaching at a school for cossack and native children. He was penniless; his salary from the Academy had been withheld, under the belief that all the members of Bering's expedition had perished, and in his straitened circumstances he could no longer afford his *slushiv* Lepekhin. Young Thoma pleaded to be allowed to work for him without wages, but Steller was too proud to consider the offer. "No, Thoma, I have no right to accept such a sacrifice. You have given me your comradeship and that is enough."

In the spring he embraced the loyal cossack and bade him farewell, and left Bolsheretsk alone. For a year he traveled through upper Kamchatka, collecting botanical specimens and making field notes, working at odd jobs to support himself and living on salmon and wild berries. The region was inhabited by fierce savages called Olyntorts, who were waging a sort of guerrilla war with the Russian provincial government, but Steller was hospitably received and spent part of the winter with them.

His crusading spirit had not been lost, and he was still enraged at the callous exploitation of the natives by civic authorities. On his return to Bolsheretsk in 1744, he accused Midshipman Kmetevski, the ranking naval authority, of mistreating and abusing the Kamchadals, and addressed a complaint to the Imperial Senate in St. Petersburg. Kmetevski revenged himself by informing the Senate in turn that Steller had liberated some natives who were conspiring to rebel against the Russians. The Senate, remembering the previous uprising of the Kamchadals and Koryaks at the time of Bering's expedition, was disturbed by this grave accusation of treason, and a courier was dispatched to bring Steller to Irkutsk for trial.

Meantime Steller had sailed from Bolsheretsk on the annual supply ship, arriving at Okhotsk in late August. He made his way north through Siberia, wintered in Yakutsk, and the following May set out for Irkutsk. The Senate's charges against him were waiting there, but Vice Governor Lange, after hearing Steller's story, acquitted him unconditionally and forwarded a full exoneration to St. Petersburg. The governor's dispatch was delayed by local officials, and did not reach the Senate until August of 1746.

Steller had traveled as far as the northern outpost of Solikamsk, and was busy investigating the flora of the Ural Mountains, when the courier from the Senate arrived with orders to place him under arrest and bring him back to Irkutsk at once. Steller was outraged that a member of the Academy should be apprehended like a common thief, and protested heatedly that he had already been exonerated by Vice Governor Lange. The courier had his instructions, and gave him twenty-four hours to get ready. He worked without sleep to organize his botanical collection and arrange for it to be forwarded to the Academy, and wrote his plaintive *Pro Memoria*, a last will and testament. Perhaps he had a premonition that he would not live long. In the morning he left with his guard to retrace the hundreds of miles back through Siberia, fuming with indignation at his ignominious treatment.

Cold weather was setting in, the rivers were frozen, and they stopped at Tara to prepare for winter travel. There another Senate courier caught up with Steller, and delivered an official dispatch explaining apologetically that the delayed exoneration had finally arrived, and freeing him to return to St. Petersburg by any route he desired. He hired post-horses and a sledge, and left immediately for Tobolsk.

Steller had always been a moderate drinker, but his arrest and subsequent reprieve had been a severe emotional strain, and he sought relief in vodka. At Tobolsk he spent three weeks celebrating his release, indulging to such a degree that he contracted a violent fever. His companions urged him to remain in Tobolsk until he regained his health, but Steller was determined to return to St. Petersburg and justify himself, and he refused to listen. Early in November he crawled into his sledge and ordered the Tatar driver to hurry south. He was burning with fever, and plied himself with vodka during the journey until he fell into a drunken stupor. They halted for food at a roadside hostel, but the driver could not arouse his sodden passenger, and left him in the sled in subzero weather while he tarried indoors over his meal. By the time they reached Tyumen, 170 miles away, Steller was dying.

Two naval surgeons, who happened to be stopping in Tyumen, worked in vain to save him. Like Bering, his will to live was gone. He was convinced by now that his career had been a failure, and all his work as a naturalist had come to nothing. He had hoped that his discoveries in America would bring him world recognition, but the manuscripts written on Bering Island, which he had forwarded to St. Petersburg, had not even been acknowledged. The only result of the expedition had been to open the Aleutians to the ruthless fur-hunters, the *promyshleniki*, who would plunder the islands until the last sea otter herds were obliterated and the Aleut race was reduced to a few beggared remnants of a once gentle and contented people.

He died on November 12, 1746, at the age of thirty-seven, disillusioned and without friends. Since he was of the Lutheran faith, the Russian Orthodox clergy refused to perform the funeral service. The only Protestant minister in all Siberia was the house-chaplain of Vice Governor Lange in Irkutsk; he hastened to Tyumen over the snow-packed trail, and "wrapped his own red mantle about Steller's body and arranged for the burial." The local clergymen would not allow a Lutheran to be interred in the Russian cemetery, and Steller's remains were placed in a shallow trench, hacked out of the frozen ground, on a bluff above the Tura River. That night some vandals dug up his corpse, stole the red cloak, and left him naked in the snow for the dogs to devour. Sympathetic natives reinterred him after several days, and placed a heavy stone on the grave.

Twenty-four years later the noted German naturalist Peter Simon Pallas journeyed to Siberia. Pallas had been a boy of five in Berlin when Steller died, but he worshipped the memory of his brilliant fellow scientist, and had edited his manuscripts for publication. On his travels he visited Tyumen, and made a pilgrimage to the bleak burial site on the bluff. Atop it was the stone "which will be seen," Pallas wrote, "until the Tura has eaten away the high bank on the spot on which it stands, when Steller's bones will be mingled with the mammoth bones on its farther shore." There is no trace of the grave today.

PART THREE

The Plunderers

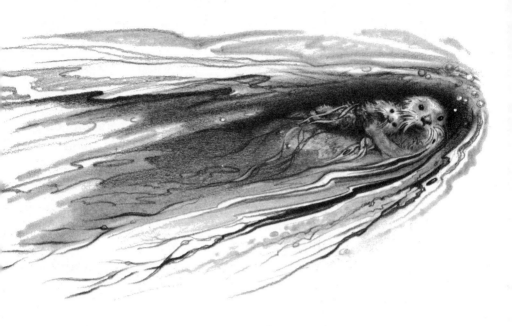

THE Second Kamchatkan Expedition might well have been forgotten, and its discoveries buried forever in the Admiralty files, had it not been for the otter pelts brought back from Bering Island. Evidence of new riches to the eastward aroused the greed of the fur-traders and their wild cossack hunters. As the quest for the black sable had enticed the *promyshleniki* from the Volga over the Urals to Siberia, so the sea otter was the Golden Fleece which lured these Russian Argonauts across the North Pacific to the Aleutians and northwest America.

In the spring following the return of the *St. Peter*, the first shipload of adventurers sailed from Kamchatka to Bering Island, returning with a cargo of sixteen hundred sea otters, two thousand fur seals, and two thousand blue Arctic foxes. Their success started a wild stampede to Alaska, greater than the Klondike gold rush which followed a century and a half later. Shipbuilding became the order of the day, though the Cossacks had no knowledge of naval architecture. Vessels were constructed of unseasoned timbers, hewn with axes from the forest. Rope had to be transported by packhorses from Irkutsk, and provisions purchased from Yakutsk at exorbitant prices. Men braved the stormy ocean in flatboats and barges and crude *shitikas*, native scows made of green planks held together with reindeer hide thongs instead of nails. The makeshift vessels were overcrowded, and so unseaworthy that they foundered at the first heavy gale, or were dashed to pieces in landing on the rocky shores.

Nothing daunted the reckless *promyshleniki*. Crews vanished without a trace in the fog, and their places were taken by other hunters, bribed by avaricious merchants to risk their lives in the frail craft. Navigation was by guess or by God. Countless numbers were lost at sea, or starved to death on the shore of some barren island, but the fever of adventure gripped them, and they forgot all caution in their lust for the velvet booty of Bolshaya Zemlya. Government officials were quick to grab their share of the spoils. The new commander at Bolsheretsk, Lieutenant Lebedef, who had married de la Croyere's widow, issued special permits to hunt in exchange for a percentage of each cargo. The Empress Elizabeth signed a royal ukase, ordering the expeditions to pay an added tribute in choice pelts to the crown.

The sea otters were taken at all seasons of the year. Hunters in leather boats would row toward a swimming otter and shoot at it with arrows, forcing it to dive repeatedly in order to prevent it from getting air. Steller had observed the "surround" method, as it was called, and described it in detail in his journal. "From the rising bubbles they notice in which direction the animal goes, while the man in the bow, with a pole to which there are fastened small crosspieces like a brush, fishes up the arrows from the water. If the animal has a young one with it, this first loses its breath and drowns. . . . Finally the mother becomes so breathless and exhausted that it cannot stay under water for a minute. They then dispatch it either with an arrow or often, when near by, with the lance." Sometimes the hunters resorted to floating dragnets of heavy twine. "When the sea otters get into the nets, they are seized with such desperation that they bite each other terribly; at times they bite off their own feet either in rage or, because they are entangled, in desperation."

In winter the otters were hunted at night on the ice drifting in from the sea, and killed with clubs. "Generally such a storm and blizzard reigns that one can hardly keep on one's feet," Steller recounted, "but nevertheless the hunters do not hesitate to use the night time. They run along on the ice without heed, even when it is drifting and being lifted on the waves to such an extent that they appear now to be on a mountain and then to plunge into an abyss. Each man has a knife and a stick in hand, and long snowshoes laced to his feet, to which are attached bone hooks or horns to prevent sliding on the ice or falling from it where it piles up. The skins must be taken off immediately, and in this the Kamchadals are so skilful that they often flense 30 to 40 in two hours. If luck is with them they bring these spoils on land; sometimes, however, when the ice is being driven completely away from shore, they must abandon everything in order to save themselves. In that case they tie themselves with a small rope to their dog, which by swimming faithfully drags them to shore."

The native Aleuts resented the encroachment on their ancestral hunting grounds, and tried to repel the invaders with primitive weapons and stones. In 1745 a large *shitika*, under command of an infamous adventurer named Chuprov, sailed to the island of Agattu, second westernmost of the Aleutian chain, and was met by a hundred natives armed with bone-pointed spears. Pipes and tobacco were offered as gifts by the landing party, but the Aleuts demanded one of the Russian muskets and attempted to seize the boat. Chuprov ordered his men to fire; one bullet pierced the hand of a native, and as the blood spilled onto the sand "his comrades threw off their garments, carried him into the sea, and endeavored to wash off the crimson stain." The long era of violence had begun.

Unable to hunt on Agattu because of the hostile inhabitants, Chuprov sailed to Attu, where he was made welcome by the unsuspecting natives and given food and shelter. The Russians repaid their hospitality by provoking a quarrel with a group of islanders, accusing them of stealing an iron bolt. Fifteen natives were slain in cold blood, and their women seized and raped. When one of the cossack crew protested to Chuprov at this wanton brutality, the commander "said nothing, but merely sent the butchering party more powder and lead."

Island by island the *promyshleniki* devastated the peaceful Aleutians, financed by enterprising merchants from as far away as Moscow. One *shitika* brought back 683 otter skins, all from Bering Island; another reported over 1000 sea otters and 2000 fur seals stowed in its hold. A fur trader from Irkutsk obtained a monopoly to hunt on Bering Island, agreeing to pay into the imperial treasury one-third of the profits; his official inventory listed 790 sea otters, 7004 blue foxes, and 2212 fur seals. Other companies received royal permission to fit out expeditions to "such islands as had not yet been made tributary," and carried their raids still farther east. Their reward was prodigious — the cargo of a single vessel was valued at 178,268 rubles — and traders became rich overnight. Andrei Tolstykh, the most capable navigator of his time, took the amazing total of 5360 sea otters from Attu alone. The island of Adak, where Chirikov had watered, yielded 820 otter skins, 1900 blue foxes, and 7000 fur seals. Three vessels sailed from Othotsk to Tanaga Island, never before visited by white men, frightened off the natives with a discharge of firearms, and came home with over 3000 sea otter pelts.

Inevitably the herds dwindled. In 1756, fourteen years after Steller had recorded the vast numbers on Bering Island, Tokstykh wintered at the site of the old camp; but though he was still able to obtain a supply of sea cow meat, not a single otter could be found. Little more than a decade of ruthless hunting had been enough to wipe out the entire population. Twelve years later, in 1768, the last sea cows on Bering Island were killed, and the species exterminated forever.

Year after year the *promyshleniki* pressed farther along the Aleutian chain, leaving a trail of devastation and death in their wake. When one island was stripped of all its otters, the plunderers moved on like a horde of locusts to ravage another. The male inhabitants of a native settlement were enslaved and forced to hunt day and night in their skin boats while the Russians lived ashore with their women. Matchless pelts were purchased for a mirror or a string of glass beads. If the islanders rebelled, they were clubbed as callously as the otters, and their villages were looted and burned. The fur stampede had become a war of invasion and conquest.

Native resistance stiffened as the *promyshleniki* encountered the more savage tribes to the eastward. In 1762, one Sergeant Pushkaref and a party of twenty market-hunters left their vessel to scour the coast in *baidars*, and landed on a previously unexplored island called Unalashka, later Unalaska. In order to safeguard themselves against attack, the hunters seized nine children from the village and held them as hostages. Despite their precaution, a band of natives ambushed the party and killed two men and wounded three others. That night they stormed the Russian encampment in force, murdering four more men and reducing the huts to ashes. The following week a pair of hunters, bathing in a hot spring supposed to cure rheumatic fever, were surprised and slain. As punishment for these outrages, Pushkaref put seven of the hostage children to death.

Since it was evident that the natives had determined on complete annihilation of the invaders, the hunting parties were recalled to the ship and Pushkaref set sail for Kamchatka with his spoils, carrying with him twenty-five young Aleut women on the pretext "that they were to be employed in picking berries and gathering roots for the ship's company." When they reached the Kamchatkan coast, fourteen of the girls were sent ashore to search for food. Two of them managed to escape into the hills, and another was killed as she tried to flee. In despair, the remaining eleven girls leapt off a cliff onto the rocky beach. Anxious to rid himself of troublesome witnesses, Pushkaref had all the other Aleut women bound with ropes and tossed overboard.

The islanders did not forget. A year later a vessel commanded by Captain Drushinnin anchored at Unalashka in the late fall, and the crew was divided into smaller groups to hunt and trap over the winter. One shore party of twenty Russians built a hut near the native village. Relations with the inhabitants appeared to be entirely friendly, and no trouble occurred until December 4. That morning five hunters set out to look after their fox traps, and Drushinnin and two junior officers paid a visit to a native dwelling. They had just entered the low aperture when they were set upon without warning by a number of Aleuts who knocked down Drushinnin and one of the officers with clubs, and finished them with some knives they had bought from the Russians the day before. The other junior officer grabbed an axe, and made such good use of it that he succeeded in reaching the winter hut alive, though mortally wounded, and alerted the rest of the party. They opened fire on the Aleuts with muskets, but one of their number, caught outside the hut, was thrown to the ground and assaulted with knives and spears until a huge cossack named Korelin, armed with a bear knife, made a gallant sortie and rescued his half-dead comrade.

For four days the Russians were besieged in their hut, unable to venture outside in search of food and water. To add to their fears, the natives displayed in plain view the garments and arms of the five hunters who had gone to visit the fox traps. During the fourth night, Korelin and three other fugitives managed to reach their *baidar* and paddled out of the harbor, the natives making no attempt to pursue them. Once out of sight of their enemies, they landed the skin boat on the beach, and set out across the island toward their ship. It was still dark when they reached the anchorage, and discharged their signal guns, but there was no reply. The sound of firing had betrayed their position to the natives, and they made a stand on top of a lone boulder, holding off their pursuers until dawn with a barrage of musket fire.

Daylight revealed an object on the beach which confirmed their worst apprehensions. It was the main hatch of their vessel, washed up by the waves onto the sand. The four trapped men made a break for the mountains, and secreted themselves in a ravine all the following day. Under cover of darkness they returned to the anchorage, and located the wreck of the vessel and the bodies of their dead shipmates strewn along the shore. Gathering a few bundles of dried fish, they stole back into the hills, hiding among the cliffs and traveling only at night. Nevertheless, they were discovered by the natives and forced to take refuge in a cave, where they held out for five weeks against repeated forays, unable to tend their wounded or bury the dead. It was not until the thirtieth of March that Korelin, the sole survivor, succeeded in signaling a *shitika* that was cruising offshore, and swam out to the small boat in a shower of arrows.

Now the islanders, thoroughly aroused, embarked on a campaign of relentless guerrilla warfare. A group of *promyshleniki* had been shipwrecked on Umnak Island, and the sixteen survivors had erected a temporary shelter of empty casks covered with sea-lion skins. During their first night ashore, a native war party approached stealthily from the sea. Their spears and arrows pierced the flimsy barricade of skins; five castaways were killed outright, and all the others severely wounded. The least disabled seized the fallen spears and launched a counterattack, driving off the savages. Three days later, a hundred and fifty islanders stormed the shelter with muskets, the first recorded instance of the use of firearms by the Aleuts. When their bullets fell short of the mark, they set fire to the dry grass in an effort to burn their quarry out.

After a month of ceaseless harassment, the castaways escaped in a stolen *baidarka* and traveled down the coast in search of help. On the beach they spotted the charred remains of another Russian vessel, and torn garments and broken lances gave evidence of a desperate struggle. They climbed the hill to the ruined encampment, and in a bathhouse discovered twenty bodies, including the ship's commander. Straps and belts tied around the necks of the corpses indicated that they had been dragged to the spot, but no further details of the massacre could ever be obtained.

Some turncoat Aleuts were bribed to join forces with the white invaders, and served as mercenary warriors when the fur-hunters encountered the inhabitants of the Shumagins and Kodiak Island. Years later an elderly native described the arrival of the *promyshleniki* on Kodiak: "I was a boy of nine or ten years, for I was already set to paddle a *baidarka*, when the first Russian ship with two masts appeared near Cape Aliulik.

Before that time we had never seen a ship; some wise men knew something of the Californias, but of white men we did not know at all. When we espied the ship at a distance we thought it was an immense whale, and were curious to have a better look at it. We went out to sea in our *baidarkas*, but soon discovered it was no whale, but another unknown monster of which we were afraid, and the smell of which [probably tar] made us sick. The people on the ship had buttons on their clothes, and at first we thought they must be cuttlefish, but when we saw them put fire into their mouth and blow out smoke we knew they must be devils.

"Among our people there was a brave warrior named Ishinik, who was so bold that he feared nothing in the world; he undertook to visit the ship and came back with presents in his hand, a red shirt and some glass beads. He said there was nothing to fear, 'they only wish to buy our sea otter skins and to give us beads and other riches for them.' The old and wise people held a council in the *kashima*, and some said: 'Who knows what sickness they may bring us; let us await them on the shore, then if they give us a good price for our skins we can do business afterward.'

"The Russians came ashore together with the Aleuts and the latter persuaded our people to trade, saying: 'Why are you afraid of the Russians? Look at us, we live with them and they do us no harm.' Our people, dazzled by the sight of such quantities of goods, left their weapons and went to the Russians with their sea otter skins. While they were busy trading, the Aleuts, who carried arms concealed about them, at a signal from the Russians fell upon our people, killing about thirty and taking away their skins. Those who attempted to escape in their *baidarkas* were overtaken by the Aleuts and killed.

"During the winter the Russians moved about from village to village. Whenever we saw a boat coming we fled to the hills, and when we returned no *yukala* [dried fish] could be found in the houses. In the lake near the Russian camp there was a poisonous kind of starfish; we knew it very well, but said nothing about it to the Russians. We never ate them, and even the gulls would not touch them; many Russians died from eating them. But we injured them also in other ways. They put up fox-traps and we removed them for the sake of obtaining the iron material."

The Russians resorted to every form of cruelty to cow the rebellious natives. Captives were knouted, blinded with hot irons, tied naked to stakes and castrated before the assembled villagers. A favorite procedure was to line up the men of a settlement in single file, and fire a musket point-blank at the first man, while the *promyshleniki* made bets as to how many in the line would be killed. The best recorded score was nine, the bullet lodging in the ribs of the tenth man.

When terrorism failed to halt the massacres, a hunter named Solovief decided to execute personal vengeance on the murderers of his countrymen. Learning that three hundred natives had assembled in a fortified *kashima*, Solovief marched his punitive force to the village. The Russians were greeted by a shower of arrows from every aperture, but when the defenders discovered that enemy bullets could penetrate their fortress with ease, "they closed the openings, took down the notched posts which served as ladders, and sat down to await their fate." Unwilling to expose his men in a frontal attack, Solovief dispatched some Aleuts to place bladders filled with gunpowder under the log foundations, and touched them off with musket fire. Those natives who survived the explosion and tried to surrender were hacked to death with bayonets and sabers.

The *promyshleniki* were constantly searching for new hunting grounds, hitherto undisturbed by man. In the spring of 1768 Fleet Master Gerassim Pribilof, cruising north of Unalashka in the Bering Sea, sighted the high cliffs of an unknown island which he called St. George, after the saint of the day. It was the southernmost of the famous group of fur seal islands which bear Pribilof's name today. The shores swarmed with sea otters, as fearless as those which Steller observed on Bering Island during the first winter; large packs of walrus basked on the ice floes; arctic foxes were so tame that they could be caught by hand. With the approach of summer the fur seals returned to their rookeries in countless numbers, the largest concentration anywhere in the world. In his first year, Master Pribilof obtained forty thousand seal and two thousand otter pelts, fifteen thousand pounds of walrus ivory, and "more whalebone than his ship could carry."

Rumors of the untold wealth in furs to be found in northwest America had spread abroad. When Captain Cook visited Prince William Sound, on his third voyage around the world, his sailors traded iron nails for a fortune in sea otter skins. Yankee market hunters came from as far away as Boston to join in the fur stampede. Spaniards pushed northward out of Mexico along the California coast, gathering pelts to send to China in exchange for quicksilver for their Mexican mines. In 1804 a single ship under Commander Baranof sailed back to Russia with a cargo of fifteen thousand pelts.

For the first third of the nineteenth century, sea otter hunting was the most important industry on the Pacific coast. The animals were so thick in San Francisco Bay, according to early records, that men in small boats could knock them on the head with their oars; the toll in the Bay averaged eight hundred a week. As the hordes were decimated, rivalry among the hunters became all the more keen. Ten years of competitive killing exterminated the entire otter population in the San Francisco area; within a few more years, the species had ceased to exist anywhere on the American mainland. By 1830 — less than a hundred years after Bering's voyage — sea otters had become so rare in Alaska and the Aleutians that Baron von Wrangell, of the Russian American Company, persuaded his government to forbid the use of firearms and protect the remaining animals by rigid conservation measures.

This brief period of respite for the beleaguered otters ended in 1867, when the United States purchased Alaska at the bargain price of two cents an acre. Ignoring the Russian ban on firearms, American hunters substituted high-powered rifles for native arrows and spears. The waste was appalling. Men patroled the beaches, aiming through telescopic sights at a swimming otter's head and trusting to luck to find the body later if it washed ashore. Countless wounded animals, shot at too great a distance from land, sank and were never recovered. When the American government sought to restrict the taking of sea otters to the natives of Alaska, white men married Aleut women and claimed the right to hunt. By the turn of the century, the islands had been stripped clean. In 1911, a fleet of thirty-one schooners combed the former hunting grounds in vain. Their total kill for the summer was a dozen skins.

That year an international treaty to protect the species was signed, and the Aleutians were declared a Federal Wildlife Refuge. Protection had come too late. Each year the otter count grew smaller, its decline speeded by Russian and Japanese poachers who continued to slip into the remote bays, unobserved in the fog, and slaughter the few isolated survivors. In 1925, an exhaustive survey failed to detect a single otter, and the species was declared extinct.

Six years later Frank Dufresne, soon to become director of the Alaska Game Commission, made a routine inspection tour of the islands in a trading vessel named the *Aleutian Native*. The trader touched at Amchitka Island, midway down the chain, and Dufresne paid a courtesy call on Chief Makary Zaochney of the Aleut village. The chief led him out of ear-shot of the other natives, and lowered his voice to a whisper. There was something he wanted to show the game man, he confided. He would call for Dufresne tomorrow at dawn, be-fore anyone else was awake.

The first gray light was showing as the chief paddled out to the *Aleutian Native*, and Dufresne lowered himself into the skin boat. They ghosted to shore, hid the boat, and the chief led the way single file across the island, his squat figure al-most invisible in the heavy fog. They came to a cove on the northern coast of Amchitka, and hid behind a boulder at the edge of the beach. As the fog thinned, the chief lifted himself to peer over the boulder, ducked down again, and gestured to-ward the water. Dufresne rose cautiously and gazed at the strands of green and purple seaweed, lifting and falling with the gentle swells. In the midst of the kelp was an unmistak-able triangular head dusted with silver hairs, moving slowly across the cove. The lone otter drifted on its back, a baby clasped in its forefeet.

America's rarest fur animal had begun its long struggle back from oblivion.

Several years after the war I revisited the Aleutians on a peacetime Air Force inspection tour. The usual solid clouds blanketed the islands, and we touched wheels on the Amchitka strip in a fog as thick as milk. Everything else had changed, since I had been stationed here during the Battle of the Aleutians, but the weather never changes. A steady drizzle streaked the windshield as we taxied to a halt before the oper-

ations building, boarded up and lifeless. The acting base commander, a very boyish-looking lieutenant, met the plane in
dripping oilskins.

"We used to have a saying in the war," I recalled as he led
me to his jeep, "that it's never too bad to fly as long as you can
see your copilot."

Evidently they still had the saying, for he gave me that
perfunctory smile which young CO's reserve for visiting colo-
nels from headquarters. "I'll show you to your quarters, sir.
They're not very much," he apologized. "Most of the base has
been closed down."

The jeep wheeled and started down the center of the abandoned runway, from which the medium bombers of the old
77th Squadron had taken off with loaded bombbays to attack
the Jap installations on Kiska. Once Amchitka was our westernmost air installation, back in the days of Alaska's forgotten
war. Maybe you never heard of the Battle of the Aleutians.
There were no headlines, no glamorous stories of dogfights
with elusive Zeroes half-rolling out of the sun. The real enemy
was the weather. Freezing clouds that loaded the wings of a
bomber with a ton of ice in less than a minute. Hundred-mile
williwaw gales that racked a fighter plane out of control and
whipped up seas so rough that a wallowing destroyer would
ship water down its stacks. Fog that wrapped the islands in a
white shroud, and socked in an airbase before the squadron
could return from a mission. No, you never read much of these
Aleutian combat pilots. Their battlefield was a rocky beach
scattered with bits of twisted metal, or a snow-covered peak
with the torn wing of a B–25 creaking in the wind, or a gray
ocean and a parachute sinking slowly in the numbing water.
Their citations read "Missing."

Now the base was condemned and in process of being
phased out. Weeds grew between cracks in the paving, and

there was no sound of revving engines in the empty parking areas and revetments. We drove past echoing warehouses and hangars, past row on row of rusting tractors and trucks — it would have been too expensive to ship them home — and past the ghostly Quonset huts, their floors ankle-deep in silt. A few faded pinup girls pasted on the curving walls were the only reminder of the leather-jacketed crews who used to sit around the smoking oilstove and play red dog and wait for the fog to lift so they could fly another mission.

Even the waterfront was deserted, curtained with eddying mist, as silent as it had been that morning in 1931 when Frank Dufresne had crept across Amchitka and discovered the last remaining otters in this same cove. To make conversation, I asked: "I don't suppose you ever heard of an animal called the sea otter?"

The lieutenant looked surprised. "Sea otter? Sure, there's lots of them here."

Obviously he was mistaken. Had it confused with the hair seal, no doubt. He saw my skeptical smile.

"We've got half an hour before mess. If the Colonel would like to see for himself, we can drive down to the pier. There's always a few playing around."

The jeep rattled over loose planks to the end of the pier, and the lieutenant jumped out and slammed the door, making no effort to be cautious, and clumped in heavy combat boots to the edge. He pointed down casually at the water.

"There's one now."

Below me, less than a dozen yards away, an otter was slumbering on his back, anchored in place by a strand of kelp looped around his middle. The forefeet, like kitten's paws, were folded placidly on his chest, the rear flippers locked behind him. Now and then a long swell would rock him in his sea hammock, and I could see the water wash through his dense mummy-brown fur. His face was wrinkled in a quizzical half-smile.

"Hello, Oscar," the lieutenant called. He explained to me: "His name is Oscar."

The otter opened his eyes and gave us an irritated glance, like an elderly clubman aroused from his noonday nap by some roisterous younger members, and backed away slowly, puffing out his mustache. Abruptly he swirled and plunged below the surface, reappearing a moment later with a sea urchin held between his paws. He cracked the spiny echinoderm and held it to his mouth, revolving it as a squirrel would a nut and spitting out bits of pink-and-green shell. As he munched, he continued to back across the harbor, leaving a trail of shell particles like peanut husks in his wake.

Oscar was the squadron favorite, the lieutenant told me at mess. When he was a yearling, a group of airmen had found him trapped in the pilings under the pier. Apparently he had drifted too close while asleep and, as the tide lowered, his head had become wedged between two supports. His struggles to free himself only tightened the vise, and he was almost strangled when they discovered him. An eager sergeant, ignoring the razor-sharp barnacles, shinnied down the piling and fastened a rope around him, and his companions hoisted the half-dead animal onto the pier. They wrapped him in a blanket and rushed him to the Air Force dispensary, and the flight surgeon gave him a shot of stimulant. The sergeant held him in his lap and tried in vain to feed him sardines and canned milk, and even offered him a piece of chocolate. After an hour he began to revive, and by the end of the afternoon he was so spry that he bit his benefactor through the blanket. The sergeant put him down, and he flopped clumsily across the floor, seeking to return to his natural environment. Reluctantly the airmen carried him to the beach, and slid him into the water. He swam a few yards, paused to look back at them, and then slowly paddled away into the fog. The sergeant swore that he saw Oscar turn once more and wave a grateful paw.

"The men all make pets of them," the lieutenant added. "There must be a couple of thousand around the island now."

It was true. The sea otter had not only survived the war, it had prospered. Perhaps the presence of the Air Force garrison had prevented foreign poachers from raiding the breeding grounds. Perhaps the airmen at this lonely outpost, won by the otter's human characteristics, had made it their business to see to its care and protection. The military, so often accused of despoiling a countryside where it is based, had brought back this shyest of wild creatures to something like its former numbers on Amchitka's serrated shores.

In every sheltered bay and inlet, as I explored the island, otters were feeding or sleeping or sporting in the breakers, as playful as children. I saw one double up, grip his hind flippers with his forepaws, and somersault over and over in sheer exuberance. Another pair seemed to be engaged in what I suppose could be called otter polo, wrestling and ducking one another beneath the surface. A youngster I observed had invented a game of his own: he would tread water in a narrow space between two rocks until a heavy swell poured through the gut, shoot the chute gleefully on his back, and swim back to await the next wave. They would dive for sea urchins in the heaviest surf, and they were fastidious feeders. I watched an otter finish a meal, roll over in the water to wash the crumbs from his chest, and then grab a slippery piece of kelp and soap himself thoroughly, rubbing the seaweed over his stomach and beneath his arms and finally lifting his flippers so that he could scrub between his legs and under his rump.

Now and then a female would drift past me with her single offspring, which she cradled in her forepaws or lugged under one arm like a football, making a curious mewing sound. The adult sea otter has a harsh catlike whine, but the cries of the young resemble those of a human infant. Otters are devoted parents; an airman insisted to me that he had heard a mother crooning a lullaby to her baby as she rocked it on her chest. I recalled an entry in Steller's journal, describing two little otters which had been carried off for food: "The mothers followed me at a distance, calling to their young ones with a wailing voice. When the young heard their mothers' voices, they wailed too. After eight days I returned to the same place and found the two females still at the spot where I had taken the young, bowed down with the deepest sorrow. Their skins hung loose and they had grown so thin that in one week there was nothing left but skin and bones."

The rate of increase in the two decades after the war has been prodigious. Today there are more than five thousand otters on Amchitka alone, and they have reestablished themselves around Kiska, and down the island chain as far as Attu. The latest official count of the Fish and Game Department estimates approximately thirty thousand in Alaska. "The sea otter could again become an important part of our coastal fauna," the California Museum of Vertebrate Zoology has stated. "The conditions for subsistence remain about as favorable, except for the presence of the human hunter, and his activities could be regulated."

Its food supply still exists in abundance. Its original habitat in the Aleutians is virtually the same as in Steller's time. Perhaps for once, with proper conservation measures, we can reverse our long sad history of despoliation and plunder, and restore this shy and beautiful animal which, in the words of Alaska's first naturalist, "deserves from us all the greatest reverence."

Bibliography

THE STORY of Bering's voyage across the uncharted North Pacific in search of Bolshaya Zemlya might have been imagined by Dampier or Daniel Defoe; but everything in this book is factual. Some of it is based on the log of the *St. Peter;* some on Lieutenant Waxell's memoirs written long after the expedition; but most of it follows Steller's own contemporary journal and, as far as I have been able, is told in his own eloquent words.

In conclusion, I should like to acknowledge those reference sources which were particularly helpful to me in my research:

BOOKS:

Bering's Voyages by F. A. Golder, in 2 volumes; American Geographical Society, New York, 1925.

Russian Expansion in the Pacific, 1641-1850 by F. A. Golder; The Arthur H. Clark Company, Cleveland, 1914.

Georg Wilhelm Steller by Leonhard Stejneger; Harvard University Press, Cambridge, Mass., 1936.

The American Expedition by Sven Waxell, translated by M. A. Michael; William Hodge & Co., London, 1952.

History of Alaska by Hubert Howe Bancroft; A. L. Bancroft & Co., San Francisco, 1886.

Vitus Bering, The Discoverer of Bering Strait by Peter Lauridsen; S. C. Griggs & Co., Chicago, 1889.

The Haunted Voyage by Robert Murphy; Doubleday & Co., New York, 1961.

Peter the Great by Ian Gray, Lippincott, 1960.

Travels in Kamchatka and Siberia by Peter Dobell, London, 1830.

A Shooting Trip to Kamchatka by E. Demidoff; Rowland Ward Ltd., London, 1904.

Alaska University Anthropological Papers, Vols. 6-10, edited by F. H. West, 1957-63.
Russian America by Hector Chevigny, Viking Press, New York, 1965.
Birds of Alaska by Ira N. Gabrielson; Stackpole, Harrisburg, Penn.
Animals and Fishes of Alaska by Frank Dufresne; Barnes, New York.

MAGAZINES:

Alaska Magazine, Juneau, Alaska.
Natural History, Nov. 1956; American Museum of Natural History, New York.

MANUSCRIPT:

Steller and Bolshaya Zemlya by Winifred Williams, Wrangell, Alaska.

ABOUT THE AUTHOR

An exceptionally talented and versatile writer, Corey Ford wrote more than 500 articles and 30 books. A member of the Algonquin Circle (which included James Thurber, Robert Benchley, and Dorothy Parker), he was an early contributor to *The New Yorker* and *Vanity Fair* and wrote for the screen.

After service in the Air Force during World War II—when his first trip to Alaska took him roughly along Steller's route— he left Manhattan to settle in rural New Hampshire, where he fished, hunted, and roamed the woods in the company of his beloved setters. From his experiences and those of his neighbors came the long-running column in *Field & Stream* that chronicled the adventures of the "Lower Forty Shooting, Angling, and Inside Straight Club," an idea that had its origin at the Red Dog Saloon in Juneau, Alaska.

During Ford's many trips to Alaska he met with Clarence Rhodes, Governor Gruening, and Frank Dufresne, the first game commissioner of the Alaska Territory and the author of several books, including the natural history classic *No Room for Bears*. Frank Dufresne and his wife Klondy became lifelong friends of Corey Ford.

Jack Sampson, *Field & Stream* editor, said in the Introduction to *The Best of Corey Ford* (1975) that the excerpted chapters from *Where the Sea Breaks Its Back* were among this country's greatest outdoor writing. Corey Ford died in 1969.